BUTTERFLY

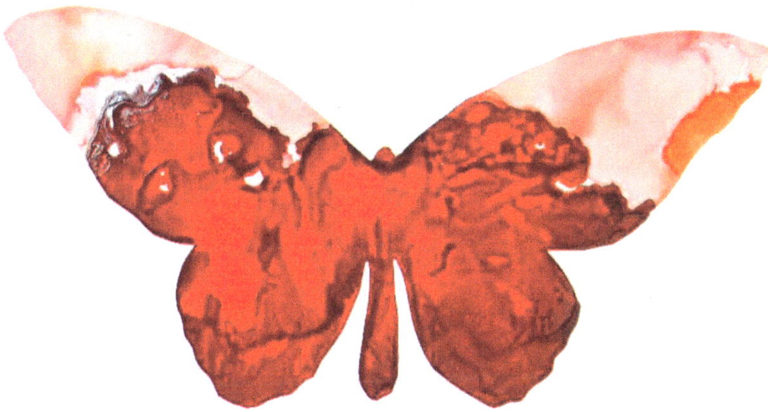

A Life, A Murder, & Beyond

The Life and Unsolved Murder of Kim Thomas

Lynn Michele Thomas & Nancy Styles Verruto

with

Emily Trask

Butterfly: A Life, A Murder & Beyond

The Life and Unsolved Murder of Kim Thomas

www.WhoKilledKimThomas.com

Published by Deux Femmes Redux

Cover Design: Michael Verruto

Cover Artwork: Ruth Ava Lyons

Interior Design: Emily Trask

First Edition

ISBN: 979-8-218-00203-9

To Elliot Roy Friedland—"My precious son, my true love!"
And to all the women, who never imagined they would find themselves fighting for their lives, facing a monster intent on killing them. And to the children they've left behind.

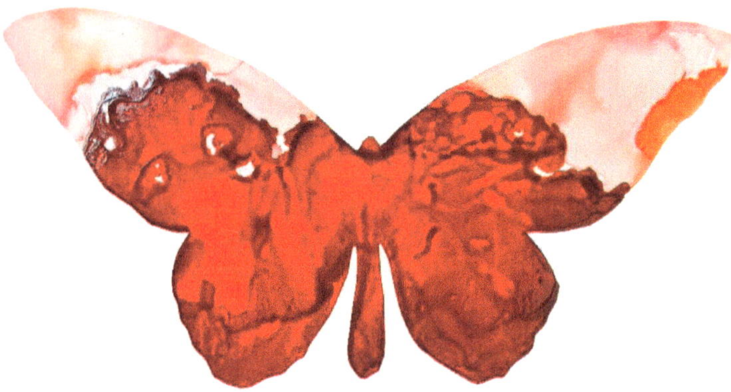

www.WhoKilledKimThomas.com

Table of Contents

Special Thanks 3

Preface 5

How to Use This Book 7

In Consideration 9

Prologue 13

Kim's Murder 17

June 8, 1990: Kim's Last Birthday 26

July 27, 1990: A Day Like Any Other… 28

A Home Becomes a Gruesome Crime Scene 33

The Shocking News 42

The Days That Followed 47

The Details of the Crime 53

Who Killed Kim Thomas? 69

In Memoriam, Kim's Life & Remembrances

Kim's Life: A Timeline 94

A Brief Life, Lived to the Fullest 98

Kim's Life in Photos 104

Adulthood and Marriage 143

Taken from Us 156

Remembrances 168

Why Kim's Story Matters 197

Afterword by Cynthia Lewis 208

In Kim's Words 211

Appendices

911 Call Transcript 222

Excerpted Autopsy Report 226

Legal Proceedings Overview 235

Who's Who 248

Crime Scene Images 254

Selected Television News Coverage 264

Selected Print News Coverage 265

Special Thanks

Charlotte Mecklenburg Police Department
Charlotte Mecklenburg District Attorney's Office
Dr. Thomas Andrew
Laura Lee Bahr
Eliza Beghe
Jan Ellen Brown
Meghan Civera
Jim Cooney
David Daniel
Sally Gordon
Edward Hinson
Melissa Kassel
Laurie Schramm Levites
Cynthia Lewis
Ruth Ava Lyons
Philip Nicholas
David O'Leary
Sherry Picker
Steve Schramm
Ellyn Silverman
Shelagh Braley Starr
Creighton Taylor
The Tamarack Writers
Carolyn G.K.H. Thomas
Joyce Thomas
Jason Trask
Tim Trask
Trask Family
Michael Verruto
Nick Verruto
Tony Verruto
Ezra Werb

Preface

Thirty-two years have passed and no one has been held criminally responsible for my sister Kim Thomas' murder. My unwavering and fervent quest for justice for Kim will only end with a conviction. The Cold Case Unit of the Charlotte-Mecklenburg Police Department (CMPD) keeps Kim's case active. There are new technologies that may help with determining the time of death and potentially uncover new evidence. Perhaps, there is someone who knows something that they have been keeping silent about all these years. Kim is gone, but she is definitely not forgotten; she left many powerful waves and ripples that are still palpable and evident every day.

~Lynn Thomas

Kim Thomas' family and friends have come together to honor Kim's life, help keep her memory alive, and find justice for her through our new organization, Deux Femmes Redux LLC, and this book. Our website www.WhoKilledKimThomas.com is a central repository for remembrances of Kim, material related to the murder investigation, and a point of contact for anyone who would like to stay up to date on the case.

How to Use This Book

Due to the nature of the subject matter of our book, the beautiful life and gruesome, unsolved murder of Kim Thomas, there are naturally many unanswered questions, moving pieces, and numerous angles to cover, which presented some unique challenges as we constructed the story.

With these challenges in mind, we structured this book in a relatively fluid way so that you as the reader can choose the way in which you approach the story. It doesn't need to be read linearly as you would normally read a book. You can start with the details of the crime and jump to the medical examiner's report. Or, you can start by reading about Kim's life from her birth through her family life and jump to the beautiful remembrances that we have captured from numerous friends and family members.

We recommend that you start with "Kim's Murder"—a fictionalized account of what Kim may have experienced in the final moments of her life—to help put the rest of your exploration in context.

You will also see when Kim's words are being used directly, they appear in Calibri font—to set those passages apart.

Throughout, you will see that we have included QR codes that you can scan with your phone, which will lead you to related interactive video or audio files, designed to enhance your reading experience and enable you to explore more about Kim's life and murder.

You can also find additional information, photos, videos, and articles on our companion website www.WhoKilledKimThomas.com.

In Consideration

Dear Reader,

As one of Kim's many friends, I feel compelled to ask something of each of you. This book you hold in your hands is an act of, and about, love.

It is a record of a young woman's life and the impact it still has on so many people, to this very day. From the beginning of her journey as a young girl, a daughter, a sister, through to marriage and motherhood. It is borne out of a deep commitment to bring the full, rich story of Kim Thomas' life to light, and share what has—and has not yet—transpired since the stunningly tragic moment when she was suddenly gone; taken without notice, warning, reason, or choice.

Now, as it is *her* story that we endeavor to share here, much of it comes from Kim's own deeply honest, creative, and sometimes painful journal entries. These were written by a young woman, in private, who likely never thought they would be shared. As such, the authors wrestled with opening such private writings for all to view. In the end, they felt sure that only Kim's own voice would give weight and authenticity, context and color to her experiences and views about life.

Further, it is a retelling, and reconstruction, too, of the time that continued after she could not. A rebuilding of the initial whirlwind of events that surrounded her death, recalled and recorded as experienced by all those who were left stunned and broken in the wake of her brutal murder, which remains unsolved as of the publishing of this very book. And of the long painful frustration, emptiness, and sorrow that a still-incomplete story brings.

It is a story brought forth from a more than 30-year-long desire by two women in Kim's life who loved her fiercely, to bring Kim Thomas, the sister, the friend, the person back into the light. And to hopefully bring some possibility for justice to bear on a still-open wound and allow the long process of healing to work toward closure.

A commitment as well is due from us all, as readers, to respect and honor the sharing of this young woman's intimate, personal voice; her naked and deep introspection into her identity, herself, her soul. We owe this sharing of Kim's soul, laid bare as it is, safe haven and care in our own thoughts, our own hearts, and our own words, as we have chosen to bear witness to a deeply private record of a person who can no longer speak for herself.

So, my request is this: Treat Kim's memories, thoughts, and voice with utmost care and respect; as you would want others to do, should they ever have reason, one day, to hold yours.

Thank you,
Kim's Friend

Prologue

"It has been said that something as small as the flutter of a butterfly's wing can ultimately cause a typhoon halfway around the world." ~*Chaos Theory*

"Happy New Year. It's 1990, and we're hoping that this next decade is a decade that's filled with joy for you," Kim says addressing her parents at the end of a home video—a gift marking the first three months of Elliot's life. But there wouldn't be a new decade for Kim. By July, she was dead.

See Kim's New Year message to her parents

On July 27, 1990, Kim Ann Thomas, at age 32, a passionate, vibrant, and loving woman was forever silenced—drained of life, her throat slashed during a horrific attack in her

Charlotte, NC, home, which she shared with her husband, Edward Friedland, their son, Elliot, and their dog, Rags. Kim Thomas has been dead almost as long as she was alive.

Her head was nearly severed from her body with more than 50 cuts to her neck, leaving intact just her spine and some soft tissue. To this day, Kim's case remains unsolved; no one has been criminally prosecuted for her murder. There are more questions than answers for those who were touched by her life … and they still feel the never-ending ripple effects of her death and her palpable absence. Any death is a tragedy for the person's loved ones, especially one so young, but an unsolved murder and an orphaned 10-month-old son add another level of complexity and heartache.

How do you measure a life—especially one that was taken in such a violent manner? With cases like Kim's, we become so focused on the circumstances surrounding the victim's death that we forget how they lived—who they were to those who loved them then and love them still.

"She was the person I loved most in the world," recalls Kim's sister, Lynn.

Kim's son, Elliot, was only 10 months old when she was murdered; he will never know just how much she loved him. And her niece, Carolyn, who shares similar mannerisms, interests, and style with Kim, will never know her stubborn, feisty, outgoing, and delightful aunt.

In a 1997 *Dateline* interview, Kim's father, Louis Thomas, shared: "The pain I feel and have suffered all these years can only be alleviated once the crime is solved. It's like a play that doesn't ever finish." Louis and his wife, Helen, both died without seeing justice for Kim.

See Louis Thomas on Dateline

With more than 30 years passing since her murder, Kim Thomas would be outraged that her killer has never been brought to justice. It's the kind of thing that would have filled her with sorrow, rage, and—most likely—moved her to action. As her sister Lynn says: "Kim had a soul large enough to feel the wrongs of others." Upon hearing about such a brutal murder of a young mother, Kim would've been horrified at the overkill and staged sexual posing of her dead body. She would have wanted to know how and why any human being would do this to another person.

Kim was physically forced to leave her son, Elliot, all alone in the world. The little baby boy who made her the happiest mother, whom she loved with all her heart, and fully intended to joyfully guide through his life.

"When she was passionate about something," says her friend Sally Gordon, "she just dove right into it." It was her role as Elliot's mother that she was most passionate about—according to many of her writings; he seemed to feed her soul. She was killed before she could achieve all that she hoped and knew that she could. She was his mom for only 10 months.

Watch home video of Elliot's first steps, May 28, 1990

Something that would've been especially difficult for Kim is the suffering of those she left behind, those whom she loved so dearly, left hurting in such unspeakable, terrible ways—and without any salve to ease their pain. If this had happened to someone she loved or even someone she may have been acquainted with, she would've done everything in her power to bring the killer to justice. The murder of Kim Thomas initially appeared to be the result of a robbery gone wrong; it has since become a case of justice gone wrong.

Kim's Murder

"I have wanted you to see out of my eyes so many times."
~*Elizabeth Berg*

It's a beautiful party. There's a diffuse, amber radiance, accentuated with shimmering candlelight, emanating from the living room. There are echoes of sparkling conversation, champagne corks popping, and ice clinking in fine crystal glasses—the sounds melding and bouncing around the room offer a kind of lull that Kim finds soothing. The occasional bellow of laughter slices through. She giggles, thinking: "That's Dad," and she beams.

Everyone is there. Mom and Dad, Lynn, Joyce, and so many other family members and friends—it's almost like everyone she's ever known is here with her now … they're all shimmering and sparkling, too.

And of course baby Elliot—the sweet little one who had made her a mother, the one she had fought so hard for. He filled her with a sense of purpose, clarity, and vision—for maybe the first time in her life. And most of all boundless, unwavering love.

An unconditional love she had never felt able to offer before. His arrival had been a dream come true.

> Joy. Joy. Elliot Roy is here at last and oh he's such a delight. He fills my days with coos and smiles and cries. He sleeps, farts, and clutches to me. I swear he cries out "Mommy"... He is my best buddy.
>
> Five weeks of my life—all of his.
> The best time of my life is NOW.

In the middle of the party guests, Elliot is perched on a blanket on the floor across the room from where she's standing. It's as if the crowd begins to part and the sounds of revelry begin to wane as he raises his arms, shaking with excitement as he looks up, and squeals. She hears: "Mommy!" His voice is filled with such exuberance and joy, she can feel her body swell with love—pure love. Reaching out her open hands to her baby to pick him up, she says: "Mommy loves you, Elliot. Yes, she does." *That word, the designation she had longed to hear—"Mommy"—maybe her whole life.*

Kim stands there motionless, holding her squirming baby, in awe of all that she is feeling. In rapt attention, she watches the scene unfold before her like a film on a screen, inhabiting and relishing this moment. It's almost as if she can actually feel the love, palpable and thick, hanging in the air like a humid, hazy summer afternoon just before the rain clouds burst and soak you through and through.

It's amazing, she thinks, all of the relationships and associations you have with people in your life—blood-related, best friend, co-worker, mere acquaintance. There are all of these connecting threads, disparate fibers between us that have brought us here together, she thinks. And maybe some have been damaged or broken, but they're still here, wrapping us in this connective web.

As she slowly turns and looks around the room, she realizes that each one of these people has helped—for better or worse—to shape who and where she is right at this moment.

> Now things can be done, undone, or not done. Now thoughts and feelings connect me with my past and future and with every other man, past and future. The stream of the unconscious at work. The river connecting all human experience. The continuity of life.

A shiver slices through her suddenly. Coldness has started to seep in. She's confused—in a sort of deja vu haze—a foggy darkness starts creeping in. *Who is this party for anyways? Is it for Elliot? For me? Eddie?* Kim moves to find her father. *Dad will know*. But she can't see him or hear him anymore. "Dad?" she calls out, but there's no response.

It's impossible to hear anything now as the drone of the party is strangely cacophonous—disquieting even. Her head is pounding with an excruciating ache.

The chill is more penetrating now. And she's starting to feel more delirious and realizes that she's no longer holding Elliot. Her head is spinning as the darkness saturates the room. *Elliot? Where is Elliot?* All the familiar, smiling faces are now blurring, fading together as a gray fog descends. "Elliot!" She cries out. She can't see him. She hears him crying but from where? Somewhere in the distance. But it's muffled. And she can hear Rags—her little Cairn terrier—barking fiercely now, too, yet he seems so far away. *Where could he be?*

"Elliot!" She cries out again with more urgency. "Eddie, where's Elliot?" Elliot's cries become more piercing. "I can't find him. I can't get to him. Do you see him? Please, someone help me!" She reaches her hands out desperately into the fog, grasping for anyone or anything, but they close on nothing.

***

Kim is awakened by a small, sharp pain in her neck. Her body jerks and she realizes she is damp with sweat. Slowly, she begins acclimating to her surroundings. *I'm in the bedroom. In bed. Safe. It was only a dream.* She's heavy with sleep, and though her earplugs are muffling the sound, she can hear Elliot's faint cries and Rags growling and barking madly from another room. For a moment, she feels relief. *I must get up and go to him,* she thinks to herself, like she had so many early mornings during the past 10 months since Elliot arrived. "Mommy's coming, Elliot," she mutters loudly. The dog needs to go out, too, she thinks, as she turns to roll from her stomach onto her left side.

But her right hand is being yanked sharply behind her back, clamped down. And then her left—her shoulders are contorted backwards and pain shoots through them. "What are you doing!?" Kim screams. "Stop!" She can feel her wrist joints popping and she struggles to free herself. But, she can't move because someone is sitting on top of her, holding her down. Her hands are now bound with something steely and cold, tight behind her back. As she writhes around, her bindings are cutting into her wrists. *Are these handcuffs?!* "No! Stop!" She screams out. "No! Let me go!"

She is wide awake now.

He's sitting on top of her. Kim feels the slice from a blade on the back of her neck.

He has a knife.

She jerks and thrashes, twisting and heaving her body upward from her stomach and hips to knock him off. *What is happening?!* She tries to slide down the bed. Elliot's cries have turned into wailing. Rags is barking like mad, but it's still muffled. *Someone is bound to hear them.* Her earplugs are still in, but she can hear everything.

She flips her body around once more. She tries to knee her captor in the groin—she twists and turns—he lets out a groan. He's thrown off and falls to the floor on the side of the bed.

Kim shrieks as loudly as she can and scrambles down off the bottom of the bed, pulling the bedding with her. Her knees smash on the smooth, cold floor with a thud.

"Help me! Somebody please! He's trying to kill me!"

She feels blood wet on her knees and strains to stand up. Kim falls again and struggles to gain her footing and balance with her hands bound behind her.

He's on his hands and knees, he's beginning to get up. Kim hoists her body up. She slips forward, almost falling again, but catches herself and stumbles toward Elliot's room. Her only thought now: *Protect my son.* But she realizes that she needs to divert the attacker's attention away from the baby. She changes course and moves toward the doorway. Her shoulder smashes against the door frame as she pushes through into the hallway. But she can feel him coming fast behind her. As she tries to run, Kim stumbles, falling on her right knee; and then she feels that hot, burning pain again, this time in the back of her neck. Kim lets out an anguished cry and struggles to her feet. "Help! Help! Somebody help me!" *Elliot.* Then another blow. This time the blade sinks deeper into her upper back and seems to suspend there for a moment. As he pulls out the knife, blood drips down her back. Kim leaps to her feet to escape another strike. The warmth of her blood is surprising as it courses down her back. She can feel her night shirt sticking to her skin on the small of her back, soaked with blood, now dripping down her bare bottom.

"Please, don't hurt my baby," she screams pleadingly. "Elliot!" she calls out. "Take whatever you want. I'll do anything." And she screams: "Just don't hurt my baby."

She moves to turn and face him, but she can't see; it's too dark. She trips backward and he's on her. Managing to maintain her balance, she knocks him off and turns toward the kitchen, almost weightless, running on her toes. He's chasing her, as she smashes through the foyer. She moves right, toward the kitchen and the back door, but the blood is gushing now and she slips forward. He's there. He grabs on to her hair tightly.

She lets out a yelp, tries to wriggle herself free from his grasp, and screams: "Why are you doing this?! Please, please, STOP! Just STOP!"

But his hold is strong and he drags her by her hair out of

the kitchen into the dining room.

"No! No! No!"

She violently thrashes her head and kicks her legs. He momentarily loses his grip. Kim lunges toward the dining room table, but slips on the oriental area rug, catching her hip on the edge of the table. She maneuvers herself around the far corner. Unsteady, her torso slams onto the table, which is covered in photographs of Elliot's first year. She can feel the piles of pictures sliding around underneath her as he presses down on top of her. And then another slash. Kim lets out an agonizing scream and smashes backward into him, managing to stand upright for a moment.

She turns again to face him, and in a sliver of a beam from the outside flood light, she squints, only to see his left arm outstretched above his head as the knife comes thrusting down to meet the front of her neck. She bellows in agony. Arms still bound behind her, she tries to turn her body, thrusting her right shoulder up in a move of protection. The knife grazes the top of her right breast. She lets out another scream.

He lifts his arm again to strike. She can see him now. "Why?! Why?! Why?!" She cries and begs. "We can work this out! I'll do anything," she shrieks. "I'll do whatever you want!" There's no response as the knife comes hammering down once more at her neck and head. Kim can feel it penetrating more deeply this time; she can hear the sound of her neck bones crunching. It's deafening as it echoes throughout her skull.

Her small body seems unbearably weighted down—like moving through warm molasses. But she tries again to turn and run. A dull thud reverberates in her head, running down her face into her eyes. She can no longer see or hold on as she falls to her knees and slips down through her blood, crashing onto her backside. Kim tries to lift herself up from her lower back and torso in an attempt to get up. He's on her again—she feels the force behind the knife as it plunges deeper.

She gurgles something inaudible, sobbing and choking on the blood now dripping down her throat. She tries to plead once more: "Why? Why? Why?" But the words won't come. She can barely hear Elliot's cries; Rags is barely audible. It doesn't matter now.

***

She *can* see him! A wave of warmth drenches her and she smiles—tears begin to form at the corners of her eyes. Kim reaches out her arms to him. *Mommy's here, Elliot. Mommy's here.*

June 8, 1990

Reflections on my life on my 32nd birthday, Kim Thomas

Overlooking our lot—a canvas with so much potential—looking through our new 'child-proof' railing—thinking about our son who is sleeping. Elliot is 9 months old today. He had a big day at the pool. He has brought joy and meaning to our lives. Eddie and I are making a haven ... a sanctuary where we can love/escape from the doldrums of the day. We are weaving a patchwork—aspects of our lives together—connected—meaningful and functional—a quilt.

Watch Kim and Elliot, June 8, 1990

Watch Kim and Elliot, June 24, 1990

July 27, 1990: A Day Like Any Other ...

"And yet to every bad there is a worse."
~*Thomas Hardy*

That last week of Kim's life at the end of July 1990 would've appeared relatively normal for a young mother with a new baby—so many exciting new experiences and *firsts*. Kim, her husband, Edward Friedland, and their 10-month old son, Elliot, had posed for professional photographs and taken their first family vacation since Elliot had been adopted in September 1989.

The night before her murder, Thursday, July 26, Kim's best friend, Nancy Verruto, recalls having a lengthy phone conversation with Kim. As they both sipped wine and prepared dinner, they discussed that Elliot had been a bit sick, but still made casual plans to meet the next day and take their children to the Jewish Community Center pool.

A little before 8:45 p.m. that same evening, Kim turned on her video camera, as she did frequently to capture various life moments. (In fact, the particular tape she used that day started at the end of May 1990 with a video of Elliot taking some of his first steps.) Fast forward to that evening on July 26: Friedland is shown wearing cloth gardening gloves, holding a small bird covered in soot, wrapped in a sheet. It and a few other birds had apparently taken up residence in their chimney. Friedland holds up the bird for the camera and says: "He's a sooty little fella." As Friedland continues outside to release it, we hear Kim say, "Aw, he's a sweetie. I hope he's big enough to be out on his own."

Kim follows Friedland outside, still filming. It's dusk, a dim light is coming through the trees, and we can see the bird is gently placed down on the deck. We hear the sounds of the woods and crickets in the background as Kim says, "Oooh, what a wonderful night."

Friedland goes somewhere off camera, and Kim walks down into the expansive wooded area beyond the deck, her little dog Rags trotting along in front of her. We hear his collar jingling. Kim, sounding concerned, says: "I hope the rest of them can get out of that chimney." There's no response. The sounds of the forest swell as she swings the camera around to the dense tree cover to capture the "wonderful night." After a few seconds, she points the camera at the base of one tree and exclaims, "A mister frog is in his home!"

We can see Rags walk over to investigate before they move back into the house. Kim repeats to Friedland, who is sitting on the couch: "I hope the rest of those birds can get out of there. Maybe we should leave the flue open?" His response is inaudible. The camera is jostled around, and at 8:46 p.m., we hear her say: "This thing is all out of tape." That was the last recorded proof of life for Kim Thomas. And no one could imagine or actually know the horror that would unfold in the hours that followed.

Watch Kim's last recorded moments

Her husband recounted that when he left the house the next morning, July 27, just before 8 a.m., Kim and Elliot were waving goodbye to him from the front door as he drove off. Kay O'Neill, who was supposed to babysit Elliot during Kim's hair appointment at 11:45 a.m., called at 8:45 a.m. to confirm if Kim still needed her. She called a total of five times, but got no response.

Nancy started calling Kim around 9 a.m., but there was no answer, which was unusual. Starting to worry a bit, Nancy made several attempts to reach Kim that morning. The answering machine was not turned on so she couldn't leave a message. Friends and family verified Kim only turned on the answering machine when she left the house, keeping it off when she was home. The answering machine was not turned on at all that day.

Nancy went to the pool in the afternoon as they had planned, and when Kim didn't show up, Nancy assumed that Elliot was probably still sick and that Kim had decided to stay home. Nancy started to head to Kim's house later that afternoon, but instead decided to turn around to finish her errands and get home before rush-hour traffic.

Kim also had plans to take Elliot to a Gymboree class at 11 a.m. right before her hair appointment at 11:45 that morning. Kim never made it to Gymboree or the salon.

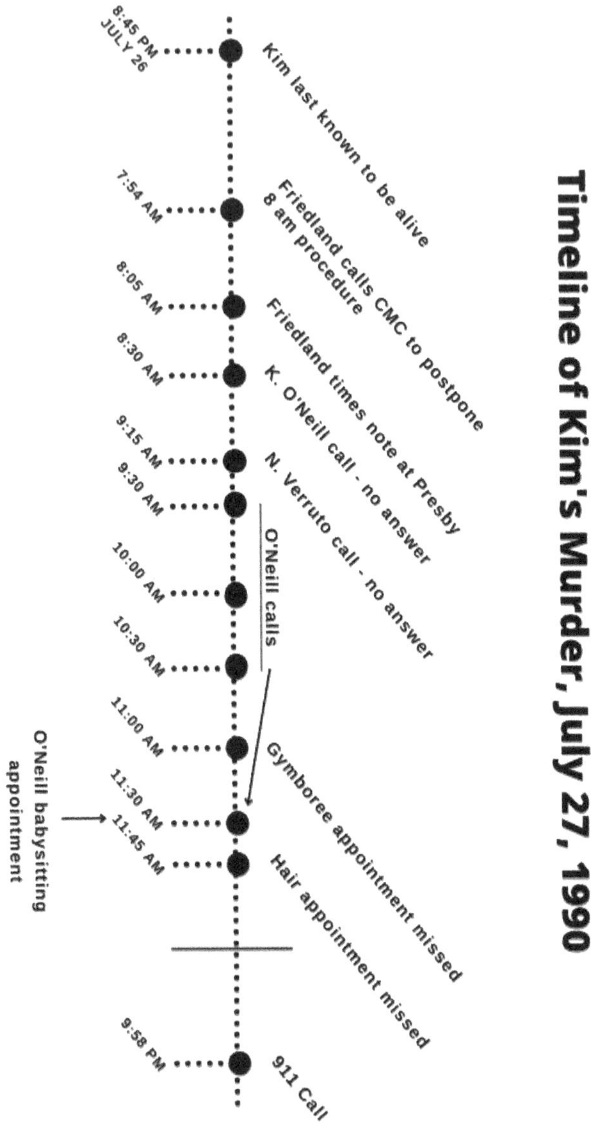

Timeline of Kim's Murder, July 27, 1990
8:45 PM JULY 26
Kim last known to be alive
7:54 AM
Friedland calls CMC to postpone 8 am procedure
8:05 AM
Friedland times note at Presby
8:30 AM
K. O'Neill call - no answer
9:15 AM
N. Verruto call - no answer
9:30 AM
O'Neill calls
10:00 AM
10:30 AM
11:00 AM
Gymboree appointment missed
11:30 AM
O'Neill babysitting appointment
11:45 AM
Hair appointment missed
9:58 PM
911 Call

A Home Becomes a Gruesome Crime Scene

"Light can devour the darkness but darkness cannot consume the light." ~*Ken Poirot*

Friedland said that as he approached the house late that evening on July 27, 1990, he thought he recalled a fluorescent light on in the front entrance area and that the baby's room was dark. Upon entering the house through the front door, he heard Elliot whining. He went first to Elliot's room. He was in his crib and had soiled himself. In an initial statement in the early hours of July 28, Friedland said:

> I walked past the front entrance and into the dining room. I did not actually go into this room when I saw Kim bound with what looks like handcuffs, her hands behind her back, blood on the floor and wall. It appeared to me that her head had been beaten…
>
> [In a written statement (signed at 12:33 a.m., 7/28/90)]

He explained later to Lynn Thomas that as a doctor he could tell she was already dead—"inert." In his statement from

August 1, 1990, he recalled that even standing at least 15 feet away from her body, he could see that she was "handcuffed and it looks like someone blew her brains out." Friedland said the handcuffs were "not like the typical two cuffs with a chain between them that you associate with the police."

He said that Kim's nightgown "was folded up in such a way that I could see her buttocks and thighs," that there was blood on the walls, and that one of the dining room chairs had been disturbed.

Friedland said that he then went back to the baby's room and then went to the master bedroom to call 911 to report that his wife had been killed. He went back to look at Kim again, and called 911 again.

9-1-1 CALL ON 7/27/90 AT 9:58 pm. Complaint Number 19900727215900

Reporting Officer P. B. Rainwater, 2688, Homicide.

TIME IS 21 HOURS, 58 MINUTES, 6 SECONDS. WILL BE THE FIRST CALL TO 9-1-1.

911 OPERATOR: (Unintelligible)

FRIEDLAND: Yeah, rush the police to my house. My wife has been killed.

911 OPERATOR: Sir, what's your address?

FRIEDLAND: My wife is dead. 38-53 Church Hill Road. Get to the house fast.

911 OPERATOR: What's your name, sir?

FRIEDLAND: Friedland. Hurry it, hurry it, it's an emergency. I'm a doctor.

911 OPERATOR: Sir, I'm dispatching right now.

FRIEDLAND: My wife is DEAD on the floor. Come here fast!

911 OPERATOR: Yes, sir.

TIME IS 22 HOURS, 5 MINUTES, 2 SECONDS. THIS WILL BE THE SECOND CALL TO 9-1-1.

911 OPERATOR: 911 Emergency, Mcall.

FRIEDLAND: This is Dr. Friedland. My wife is dead. I need help down here. I called you before.

911 OPERATOR: Wait, where are you, sir?

FRIEDLAND: 38-53 Church Hill Road.

911 OPERATOR: Church Hill Road?

FRIEDLAND: Yes, 38-53 Church Hill Road. I'm waiting for the police.

911 OPERATOR: Okay, sir. Have you talked with Medic?

FRIEDLAND: I spoke with police five minutes ago. Where are they? She is dead! I'm a doctor.

911 OPERATOR: All right, sir …

FRIEDLAND: I need help now!

911 OPERATOR: Sir … sir … calm down, just a minute, okay? You know … just calm down.

I'm gonna let you talk to Medic, okay? The police are on the way. Stay on … stay on the line, sir.

(Dial tone, numbers going through, phone rings)

MEDIC: County Emergency (unintelligible)?

FRIEDLAND: Yeah, this is … uh … Dr. Friedland. Listen …

MEDIC: Uh huh?

FRIEDLAND: … my wife is dead. She's been murdered in my house. Where are the police?

MEDIC: We … we have … uh … Medic and Police en route, sir.

FRIEDLAND: They better get here soon.

MEDIC: Oh …

FRIEDLAND: … because it's very difficult right now.

MEDIC: I know.

911 OPERATOR: Dr. Friedland?

FRIEDLAND: Yeah?

911 OPERATOR: Um … I'm sorry, this is 9-1-1 still on the line with you.

FRIEDLAND: Yeah?

911 OPERATOR: Um … I did not take your first call, sir, and I know you're extremely upset.

You said she has been murdered?

FRIEDLAND: Yes.

911 OPERATOR: Did you come …

FRIEDLAND: She's handcuffed and it looks like someone blew her brains out.

911 OPERATOR: Uh … sir, did you come in …

FRIEDLAND: I'm a doctor. Believe me …

911 OPERATOR: Yes, sir. Did you come in and discover the body?

FRIEDLAND: Yes.

911 OPERATOR: Okay. So there is no suspect still on the scene?

FRIEDLAND: I hope not.

911 OPERATOR: Oh, okay, all right, sir. We are on the way to you, sir.

FRIEDLAND: Thank you.

911 OPERATOR: Yes, sir.

MEDIC: Medic's in route also, sir …

911 OPERATOR: All right, thank you.

TIME NOW IS 21 HOURS, 59 MINUTES, 27 SECONDS.

[See Original Transcript on page 215.

Listen to 911 calls

In between his 911 calls, which were approximately five minutes apart, Friedland called his medical partner Dr. Kenneth Dunbar and he said, "Kim's dead." "Someone has killed Kim." Initially, Dunbar thought it was a joke, but quickly realized it was not. Friedland asked, "Can you believe it?" and then asked Dunbar to come over to help him. Friedland was standing in the doorway holding Elliot when Dunbar arrived—just before law enforcement.

Upon entering the house, Dunbar's immediate reaction was to go to Kim's body to provide aid. "You can't help her, you cannot do anything," Friedland assured him.

He handed Elliot to Dunbar and asked him to change the baby and take care of him. Dunbar reported that it took about 10 minutes to clean Elliot, who was now passive and quiet, and Dunbar recalled, maybe a little feverish. After about an hour, Dunbar took Elliot home with him. Elliot seemed very thirsty and drank three or four 4-ounce bottles.

Captain D. D. Frye, one of the first on the scene, reported Friedland was

> … carrying a baby. The man (Friedland) was very calm and he said—my wife's been brutally murdered. He wasn't excited or crying … The officer and me were asking him if anybody else was in the house and he said no. He had just gone in and seen his wife and he knew that she had been murdered.

Lynn Thomas recalls asking Edward how he knew the killer was not still in the house. He told her that "it was clear it was over." He said he just knew.

As the detectives took Friedland's statement immediately after arriving at the crime scene, Friedland continued to calmly conduct business on his phone. Within 90 minutes of finding his wife's body, he said to one of the detectives, "I have to find a way to get on with my life."

When the phone rang after 11 that Friday night, Nancy Verruto remembers getting scared. No one ever called them that late.

> We had just finished watching the movie that I rented earlier in the day. We started getting ready for bed. We turned off the lights and as we were heading to the bedroom, the phone rang. My husband, Michael, picked it up. He didn't say much. He was just listening. He had this very grave look on his face, and from what he did say, I gathered enough. Kim was dead.

Nancy recalls flying into a rage, throwing things off her dresser and screaming, "fuck, fuck, fuck." Then it all went to hell, she says.

The Verrutos got a friend to stay with their kids and headed to Kim's house. When they arrived, the whole place was fully taped off with yellow police tape. They couldn't drive down the driveway and had to walk from the gravel road. As they approached, they could see through the trees that there were a lot of flashing lights and activity, and what seemed like dozens of police cars and medical vehicles. They walked toward the house and met one of Friedland's business partners and others who were standing around.

"No one seemed to know what was going on," Nancy explains. "When I saw the coroner's van, I knew what that meant. It was Kim."

Finally, they saw Friedland emerge from the house carrying the dog Rags wrapped in a towel in his arms, walking toward them. "We each got on either side of him and literally carried him down the driveway. He was so out of it. He was like dead weight at that point," Michael Verruto recalls.

Watch Nancy and Michael tell their story

Fita Alfaro, who had worked for Kim and Friedland, heard on the news that night that there had been a murder near

Kim's address. She couldn't sleep and insisted that her husband drive her there to see if there was anything she could do. She saw Dr. Friedland at the entrance to the road leading to the home, and asked, "Eddie, is Kim OK?" He replied, "Kim is at peace now."

While standing at the end of the driveway, Friedland asked Michael to go get his mother, Josine, who lived close by. Michael remembers thinking: "How do you even tell someone that their daughter-in-law has been murdered?" Once Michael returned with Josine, they took Friedland, his mother, and Rags back to their house where Edward proceeded to tell them what had happened from his point of view.

Michael and Nancy remember him saying, "She's gone. That's not Kim in there. A monster did this … Kim is at peace now." Again and again over the days that followed, he would repeat: "A monster did this …"

The Shocking News

"Woman Found Slain In Her Southeast Charlotte Home."
The Charlotte Observer, July 28, 1990

"I will never forget when we found out," remembers Kim's cousin Jackie Orr. "My brother and I and some friends had been out that night dancing and having fun. We walked into the house and my parents were both sitting at the kitchen table—crying. And, if you knew my dad, you would understand—seeing him sitting there with big, slow, rolling tears before he could stop them was frightening. Both he and mom loved Kim so much. She was quite special. Immediately, we knew something horrible and awful had happened. We couldn't really take in or comprehend the horror of it all."

Kim's cousin Melissa Kassel recalls sitting in her apartment in Boston when her father called to tell her that Kim had been murdered. "I was in complete shock. I had just talked to her recently. I couldn't move for hours. I basically spent the next year envisioning her murder."

Then one day many years later, Melissa woke up and said

to herself: "I can't keep doing this or I will go crazy." She adds:

> I have learned to shut down my brain in regard to this. I don't think anyone understands just how much this has affected me. She was the world to me. The bottom line is that Kim should be alive. She should be on this earth.

Joyce Thomas, upon hearing the news of her younger sister's horrific murder recalls thinking:

> How horrible, tragic, and painful it must have been for Kim to realize that she was being murdered, and how awful it must have been for Elliot to hear the anguished cries of his mother as she valiantly fought for her life.

Lynn Thomas was at her boyfriend's house on Saturday, July 28, 1990, when the call came from her sister Joyce at 2:45 a.m. Her boyfriend answered the phone and said, it's your sister Joyce. "I thought she was calling to tell me about taking the Bar Examination," Lynn remembers. "Have Steven hold you," Joyce said. "Kimmie's been murdered." At one point Lynn said, "Who is this? Is this some kind of joke?" Upon realizing it was real, she was numb and in disbelief.

> All I could feel was rage, and denial; thinking 'no, that's not possible. Someone murdered Kimmie?' It was unthinkable. I called Dad after I spoke with Joyce, and he could barely

say the words as he held back his tears. Friedland told him: 'She was bludgeoned to death.'

When I returned home, the Waltham Police had left a note on a matchbook cover outside my door to call my dad when I got home. I immediately made arrangements to go to New Jersey to meet my parents and then to Charlotte. I was up all night and remember thinking: 'What do I wear to my sister's funeral?' It was all very surreal and time was distorted. I arrived in Newark Airport later that day, July 28. I don't remember that flight.

The first person I saw at the airport was our uncle, Eddie Kassel, Melissa's father. He had driven my parents to the airport. He immediately said to me: 'You have to be strong for your parents.' I knew what he meant: 'Do not cry,' but I couldn't stop crying. I walked up the stairs and saw my Dad buying the airline tickets. He said: 'Please don't cry.' Stunned, I sucked my sadness inside and walked over to Mom.

As we started to board the plane, Mom looked at me and said, 'Now you are my baby.' We had three seats in a row at the back of the plane. I was crying and the flight attendant asked me if I was scared to fly. I said 'no' and told her that my sister had just been murdered in Charlotte. She didn't know what to say or do, but she offered us free drinks and shortly afterwards returned and offered us seats in the first-class section since no one was sitting up there.

I remember being so enraged at my dad that he was reading *The New York Times*. I wanted to scream at him, 'What is so important in that goddamn newspaper than Kim's murder?!' At some point, I realized that is how he dealt with his feelings: Get buried in the news of the day.

Mom confided in me that she thought Elliot had also been murdered but that no one wanted to tell us.

After arriving in Charlotte, we headed to Josine's, Edward's mother's apartment. Edward was there and Dr. Dunbar, his partner, brought Elliot over shortly after we arrived. The first thing Josine said to me is: 'Kim loved you so much.' The rest of the time is a blur. The priest came, and others, and eventually we, my parents and sister Joyce, checked into the Hyatt Hotel.

When we went to have dinner that night, my sister Joyce said, 'there will never be five of us again for dinner'— a reference to our regular Sunday family dining experiences when an

> extra chair needed to be added to the end of the table to accommodate the five of us.
>
> The next day, I remember Joyce called the medical examiner and she was told that Kim's throat had been slashed.

In 1991, Kim's childhood friend Creighton Taylor wrote in a letter to Elliot:

> Kim was my childhood best friend. It is a friendship, I am sorry to say, that did not continue into adulthood. I have felt closer to Kim, and reminded more strongly of her influence on my life, ever since I heard of her death. I had neither seen nor spoken to Kim in well over fifteen years, yet when I got a phone call from my mother telling me she was gone, I dropped the phone, stopped breathing, and felt overcome by shock. Kim gone? Kim dead? Even as I sit here to write this, I find myself with tears in my eyes, still disbelieving.
>
> [See the full letter on page 180.]

The Days That Followed

"Slaying Chills Southeast Neighbors … As Son Cried, Activist Found Beaten in Home."
The Charlotte Observer, July 29, 1990

"We were all in shock that night," Nancy Verruto explains. "We brought Eddie, Josine, and Rags back to our house. We sat in the small den, shocked, sometimes silent, sometimes listening to him speak. We talked essentially throughout the entire night. He spoke of the monster that did this. And said things like 'they're not going to win.' That he and Elliot had to move back in to show them that they didn't win. They had to take back the house and take back their ground. He spoke of having to get back in the house as soon as possible and getting their lives back to normal, to prove that whoever did this didn't win. He said he was going to get a gun to protect himself and Elliot. There was a lot of ranting about things like:

> 'Maybe Elliot and I should leave Charlotte, and I can just be a simple country doctor.'

> 'Kim and I moved here to get away from violence like this.'
>
> 'Charlotte was supposed to be safe.'
>
> 'How can we stay in this city with this horror over us?'
>
> 'But if we leave, whoever did this would have won. We can't go.'

Nancy recalls: "He told us that Kim had obviously been hit on the head with a blunt object of some type. He wasn't sure what the object was, but was fairly certain that her head was 'bashed in,' her skull crushed, and her head severely damaged, as there was blood all over her head. Eddie went over again and again how Kim's hands were tied behind her back with some kind of a contraption."

He told the Verrutos and Lynn Thomas that he was certain that they were not real handcuffs, "but some kind of contraption that someone would have rigged in their garage or something from a farm." He said it was not rope, but metal or wire, but he was adamant that they were not handcuffs—"maybe baling wire." He described how she was face down in a pool of blood—"there was blood everywhere—she was murdered. Blood on the walls … dining room furniture knocked around. "Josine was hysterical the whole time," Nancy remembers.

> Every time she would hear him talk of anything about Kim, she would sob. He would try to calm her down and say that he 'wasn't going to do anything stupid,' but he 'wasn't going to let them win, that he and Elliot were the victims.'

At some point, Nancy asked him what he did first when he got home that night. She recalls that Friedland said he was angry because he had called Kim twice that day and she did not answer. He walked in the house, calling for Kim. It was dark, he said, all the lights were off. He was pissed and thought that she may have been drunk. He told them: "I walked right in the house, heard Elliot crying, turned toward the bedroom, opened the door, and went and picked up Elliot—he was covered in shit." Friedland said he was even more pissed then. He then walked out into the hallway and saw Kim in the dining room, stared at her for a number of seconds, and then called 911.

As the sun was rising, the Verrutos remembered that they started talking more about next steps. Friedland said that he needed to get back in the house and get his life back to normal:

> 'I wonder how the cops are doing? They haven't called us all night.'
>
> 'They know where we are, right?'

> 'I'm getting concerned. I'm going to drive over there to see what's happening and get some clothes for us.'

Michael also remembers discussions where it seemed Friedland had confidence in the police with statements such as:

> 'They [the police] say that crimes like this are solved within the first 12 hours or so … after that it gets harder to catch them, so let's hope they can get it done.'
>
> 'They seem to have some good leads.'

Nancy remembers that after Friedland got off the telephone with the police that morning, he told them that the police would not allow him into the house to retrieve items for Elliot and him. Michael suggested that he call Charlie Barkley, who was the business attorney for Friedland and the Verrutos. He recalls:

> We thought that maybe Charlie, who was related to the sheriff of Mecklenburg County, might be able to get him into the house or at least know how to deal with the police in this kind of situation (not in an elusive way but as a matter of protocol). He then called Charlie who came to meet with Edward at our house. At the same time, we were making arrangements for Nancy to pick up Elliot from the Dunbars.

> Sometime that day, we all ended up at Josine's apartment. Helen and Lou [Thomas] were asking us to help them with some arrangements for Kim because we were Catholic. They needed advice on churches and priests in the area. They made arrangements for the priest to come and meet with them that afternoon at Josine's. Elliot was with us.

Nancy recalls that Friedland arrived later, and upon seeing Kim's family, let out a moan, began to cry, and started to fall to the floor. Michael caught him, pulled him up, and held him while he cried for a moment. He was asking pleadingly: "How are we going to survive this?" And then while holding Elliot, he started talking about how they were the real victims here. "Kim is gone. She doesn't feel anymore. It is over for her. We are the real victims here because we must continue on with this pain." He would repeat these sentiments over and over, for months, both Nancy and Michael recount, and that he spent long hours over the next few days talking with his sister Lesley in their guest bedroom.

For the first few weeks after Kim's murder, Friedland was at the Verrutos house frequently. One night, he asked Michael to come outside for a walk to talk. As they walked around the block, Friedland said that over the next few weeks some distressing or upsetting news might be coming out about him and/or Kim. He had reason to be concerned for his own life and that there were *people* out to get him.

Michael asked him who these people were, but he wasn't sure … he didn't elaborate. He was scared that he might be killed and that *they* (Michael assumed he was referring to the police, as by this time, the police had made it clear that they considered him a prime suspect) would say that he killed himself and therefore proven his guilt—committing suicide because he was unable to live with the crime he committed. Friedland told me that "if we were to be told of his *suicide* we should not believe it … and check it out … and tell the authorities about this very conversation." Michael recounted all of this to Nancy after Friedland left that night.

The Details of the Crime

"Every true crime story is actually true for someone."
~*Charles-Haden Savage (played by Steve Martin), Only Murders in the Building*

Kim's murder at first appeared to be the result of a robbery gone wrong, but it was soon determined that nothing was taken from the home. Kim's purse was on the doorknob with her billfold visible, which held a substantial amount of cash and credit cards. Kim was still wearing a diamond pendant, diamond earrings, and a gold bracelet. Kim's wedding band was the only item that was missing—it has never been recovered. The killer rummaged through many items in a few areas of the house without taking anything, returned everything to its original place, closed the drawers and doors, and turned off the lights.

In testimony during Friedland v. City of Charlotte, CMPD Investigator Donald Rock testified:

> Something didn't fit because the house had not been ransacked. There were a lot of items there which typically if a burglar had come in

> he could have stolen, items, small TVs, small stereos, things of that nature. They were all in place. Nothing was missing … the house was—was extremely neat, nothing out of place, which—which struck me as odd.

There was no evidence of forced entry and the home's security system was proved to be working—though it was not on. The investigators postulated that it was unlikely that Kim Thomas would have voluntarily allowed another person into her house while she was in her pajama top, was not wearing any underwear, and was wearing earplugs. The only possible point of entry for an intruder was through the side door to the kitchen that was found closed but unlocked.

The killer's footprint path and luminol testing indicated that he first went to the master bedroom. Investigators concluded that Kim was likely first assaulted when she was asleep. Evidence indicated that Kim was probably sleeping on her belly—her usual sleeping position according to family members.

It was likely she was handcuffed—behind her back—before she had an opportunity to fight. She had no significant wounds and no defensive wounds at all on her hands. Her fingernails were intact and her fingernail polish was not chipped or broken. At autopsy, the medical examiner discovered that while Kim Thomas' hands and arms were covered in blood, there was no blood underneath the handcuffs, supporting the fact that Kim Thomas was attacked and handcuffed before any major wounds were inflicted.

The killer made some hesitation wounds on the back of her neck with a sharp cutting tool, and then made two stabbing wounds on either side of her neck. It appeared that Kim had probably kicked him in the groin, and got up off the bottom of the bed.

Investigation further determined that she then fled across the length of the house to the kitchen, and had set one foot in the kitchen when the killer caught her by her hair and pulled her back into the dining room. From there, the killer struggled to subdue her and inflicted the major cutting wounds. Holding Kim by her hair, the killer cut at her neck. The numerous penetrating cuts caused heavy bleeding, resulting in her slipping in a pool of her own blood and falling on her back—though she was found on her stomach. Investigators speculated that the killer turned her over onto her stomach to stage a sexual assault scene. Kim was not sexually assaulted, but her legs were splayed open as if she had been. Her white silk pajama top, stained red with blood, was folded up in such a way to expose her buttocks.

The killing ended with Kim lying on the dining room floor with her head turned to one side. Photos of Elliot were spread in disarray on the dining room table, smeared with Kim's blood, and one photo was crumbled.

The signs of rage, fierce struggle, and overkill left what some Charlotte homicide officers would call one of the most horrific and gruesome crime scenes they had ever witnessed. Investigators told family and friends that it appeared Kim had "fought like a tiger," desperately trying to escape her attacker, repeatedly trying to stand up and falling over several times, all while the killer attempted to decapitate her.

Investigators postulated that the killer locked Kim's dog, Rags, in a bathroom during the murder and had moved him and his bed into the master bedroom after the murder. The dog's bed was always kept in the kitchen according to the housekeeper and friends, never in the master bedroom.

After Kim was dead, the killer moved to Kim's office where he touched items on the desk and opened and closed the drawers of the desk, as indicated by blood impressions that appeared to be made with fabric gloves saturated with Kim's blood; however, he appeared to take nothing from the office. A filing cabinet remained untouched. He opened and closed the door to the office behind him. The killer then went back to the master bedroom, touching a number of items in Friedland's closet and bureau, again taking nothing.

Investigators concluded that the killer was familiar with the interior of the house for a number of reasons. The amount of blood and the impressions on the light switch in the master bedroom showed that the killer turned on the light when he entered the room, which may indicate that the murder happened while it was still dark outside. The blood pattern around the light switch showed that the killer turned it on and off with a flick of a gloved finger, further indicating familiarity with the layout of the home. In contrast, if a stranger would attempt to turn on an unfamiliar light, the person would *palm* the wall, searching for the light switch.

Additionally, the door to Kim's office was obscured by the door that leads from the hallway to the den. It is not visible from the front door and when the door from the hallway to the den is open to permit passage between those two rooms, the office area is not visible. The killer also did not have to "palm" the wall to locate the light switches throughout the house.
Since Friedland reported to investigators that the light was off in the master bedroom and the door to that room was closed when he came home on the evening of July 27, the killer had to have turned off the light and closed the door when he left the master bedroom after killing Kim.

Luminol testing of the master bathroom sink yielded a reaction that suggested the presence of large amounts of blood. One luminol witness exclaimed, "It lit up like a Christmas tree." The presence of blood was consistent with the killer washing blood from his hands after removing his bloody gloves. Investigator Hollingsworth explained:

> This [the reaction] was more like something was washed and you had splatter marks through the sink. Similarly, if you saw a kid with really dirty hands wash his hands in the sink and not clean the sink out, you'd have splatters of dirt and mud in the sink. This was the same type of reaction. You had droplets … a big pattern in the bottom of the bowl of the sink and then splash marks coming out, that type of reaction in luminol.

Robert Ressler, an expert who spoke on behalf of Friedland during one trial, testified:

> Keeping in mind that burglaries have to be done quickly, a burglar doesn't have the luxury of spending two or three hours looking for things. And as a result, even if it's not trashed or vandalized, drawers are pulled open, and things are scooped out on the floor or, you know, everything is disrupted … none of that searching is present here. A closet door is open, a kitchen drawer is open, an office has some blood smears [on] some paperwork. It's just not there.

No unknown fingerprints were recovered as the killer was wearing gloves. Law enforcement refer to a scene like this as an organized murder. The killer brought gloves, handcuffs, and a cutting instrument to the scene, and took everything, in addition to the sheets and duvet, when he left—except for the handcuffs. The murder was well executed, indicating it was premeditated, and that the killer was organized and intelligent, rather than disorganized or frenzied.

The killer apparently exited through the side door in the kitchen, the door closest to the area where Friedland and Thomas parked their cars.

Video from the crime scene

Time of the Murder

When the police arrived around 10 p.m., all the blood including the pools of blood around Kim were dried and caked, indicating she had been dead for many hours.

Five different pathologists, including Dr. Michael Sullivan, the medical examiner for Mecklenburg County who initially autopsied Kim's body, agreed she more likely died before 7:30 am than after. Time of death was based on rigor and livor, unanswered phone calls, missed appointments, and Kim's sleeping attire. Sullivan stated that the time of death could have been up to 16 hours prior to the body being found. Also, no food, coffee, or alcohol was found in her stomach.

During the course of that autopsy, he [Dr. Sullivan] extracted vitreous fluid from Kim Thomas' eye for the purposes of later testing. Subsequently, the potassium measured in this fluid yielded the value of 11.8. The measure of potassium in vitreous fluid can provide information about the range of time within which death occurred. Dr. Sullivan believed the condition of Kim Thomas' body, the surrounding circumstances, and the results of the vitreous potassium test supported an investigative conclusion that Kim Thomas died in the early morning hours of July 27, 1990. Specifically, Dr. Sullivan believed that 'the evidence would indicate it's more likely it [death] occurred in the early morning hours,' And the facts that Kim Thomas failed to answer her telephone or activate her answering machine 'would certainly make it much more likely that it [death] occurred in the early morning hours.' [See excerpts from the autopsy report on page 219.]

Dr. Michael Baden, New York State medical examiner, who was also the head of the medical expert team in the then-ongoing O.J. Simpson case, claimed that it was more likely than not that Kim died before 7:30 a.m. As discussed earlier, in March 1995, his testimony was ruled inadmissible because he utilized criminology to form his expert testimony. In North Carolina, a physician could only testify based on medical evidence and other scientific methods. Since criminology was not considered a science in North Carolina, his testimony was ruled inadmissible.

Baden testified:

> The changes in the body that occur after death: the rigor mortis, the lividity, and the fall in body temperature, were all well-advanced when the medical examiner arrived at the scene after midnight and are consistent with death having occurred before 7:30 that morning. The vitreous potassium level in the eye was 11.8 mEq/L when drawn at the time of the autopsy later that morning. This level further indicates that Ms. Thomas had died before 7:30 a.m. … It is my opinion, based on the postmortem body changes, the eye potassium level, and the circumstances of death that it is much more likely that Ms. Thomas died before 7:30 a.m. on July 27, 1990 than after that time.

Dr. John D. Butts, MD, the chief medical examiner for the state of North Carolina, wrote:

> I would be in general agreement with Dr. Baden's conclusions, as I believe Dr. Sullivan (the medical examiner for Mecklenburg County) is. Dr. Baden did not base his opinions regarding the time of death solely on the vitreous potassium findings, but on a host of other postmortem changes and circumstantial evidence that would make it

> more likely that her death occurred at or about the time she was allegedly last seen alive than later on the day. This is a very reasonable conclusion…

On April 2, 1999, Dr. Richard P. Hudson, Jr., chief medical examiner, state of North Carolina, testified that it was reasonable to conclude that Kim Thomas was killed before 8 a.m. on July 27, 1990, based on the facts that Kim Thomas was found wearing her nightclothes, with earplugs in her ears, and her baby was found only in a diaper and had not been dressed for the day." He further testified that all of the forensic and investigative factors that he reviewed were consistent with Kim Thomas having been murdered before 8 a.m.

Upon reviewing Kim Thomas' autopsy reports in 2021, Dr. Thomas A. Andrew of White Mountain Forensic Consulting Services, sheds more light on the time of death based on updated forensic pathology literature.

> Time since death or postmortem interval (PMI), while difficult to estimate, is often a critical issue in unwitnessed violent deaths. While there are a number of objective physical findings upon which forensic pathologists rely, including classic early postmortem changes of the body, the forensic pathologist does not typically interpret these findings in a vacuum, but puts them in the context of the historical circumstances

surrounding the death revealed by various investigative sources. Reliance on postmortem changes alone would confine the PMI estimate in this case to a broad range of as little as 12 to as much as 36 hours from the time of her postmortem examination. By the clock, this would be between 20:45 on 7/26 to 20:45 on 7/27. Investigative details of Ms. Thomas last known to be alive at 20:45 on the 26th and her failure to respond to phone calls and missed appointments commencing at 08:45 on 7/27 narrows the window of time to between 24 and 36 hours, or between 20:45 on 7/26 and 08:45 on 7/27.

Dr. Baden's insistence on the importance of the drying of the blood at the murder scene was well-placed, but at the time could not be supported by the literature. More recent forensic science research has addressed this issue, so often an important factor at crime scenes. Blood deposited on surfaces outside the body has been found to undergo a predictable sequence of events to the point of drying, consisting of five stages: coagulation, gelation, 'gel-solid mixing,' solid and final desiccation. A 2020 Chinese forensic study demonstrated time frames for each stage:

Coagulation (0-4.5 h)
Gelation (>4.5-20.0 h)

> Gel-solid mixing (>20.0-37.0 h)
> Solid (>37.0-40.0 h)
> Final desiccation (>40.0-45.0 h)
>
> This is important information in that, by all accounts, there was no visibly fluid blood at the scene when Friedland reported the murder at 21:58 7/27 or when an investigator was at the scene at 02:00 on 7/28. Thus, all things considered, Kim Thomas was murdered very late on the 26th or early the 27th, far more likely than not, before 7:30 a.m."
>
> In summary, the autopsy and investigative evidence reliably establishes the time of death of Kim Thomas in an interval between when she was last known alive at 20:45 on 7/26 and the early morning hours of 7/27." Based on these results, he estimated Kim was murdered between 2 a.m. and 4 a.m. on July 27.

The Brutality

Kim's autopsy revealed that she was cut many times with a "small, sharp cutting instrument." DA Richard Gordon told the Thomas family that Kim's head was only "hanging on by her spinal cord and a few pieces of soft tissue." Special Agent Cooper commented in a deposition for Friedland's malicious prosecution case against the Charlotte Police Department that the "level of comfort and familiarity that the offender (sic exhibited) at the crime scene"—amount of time he spent in the house, for example, and his evident "lack of panic"—suggested a "personal" motive, "one which reflects a deep degree of animosity, anger, and frustration." [See Malicious Prosecution Case: Edward Friedland v. Four Detectives and City of Charlotte, page 231.]

Dr. Baden commented:

> My evaluation and assessment as a forensic pathologist I suspect would be the same as yours in that the pattern of injuries [would] be overkill. The injuries, the unnecessary injuries you know after she's dead. And there are a lot of those that would indicate a close emotional involvement; that is, the first person I would think of would be a spouse and somebody who had so many excessive injuries and more than necessary to cause death.

As mentioned earlier, "Kim's body looked staged—manipulated to seem as if she suffered a sexual assault (though she did not)," wrote Cynthia Lewis in "Either/Or." [Lewis, Cynthia. "Either/Or." *Charlotte Magazine*, May 31, 2006]

Dr. Sullivan in testimony agreed: "There was no evidence of sexual assault—just anger, rage, and a clear intent to make sure that Kim Thomas was dead."

The Profile

The FBI Behavioral Science Unit (BSU) studied this crime according to information provided to them by the Charlotte Police Department, the medical examiner's report, Kim's journal, and television interviews. No opinion was drawn as to whether Friedland was the person responsible for the crime, but he could not be eliminated as a possibility. There was a lot of rage and anger evident at the crime scene, but there is no way to tell whether it was generated at the crime scene or brought to the scene.

The BSU assumed that the primary motive for the crime was anger or revenge, and concluded that the assailant would probably be a white male with approximate age as that of the victim. The offender is probably involved in an unstable relationship with a member of the opposite sex (possibly the victim) or is currently uninvolved. The offender has probably had a series of unsuccessful relationships with women and possibly may have been involved with domestic violence. The educational level of the offender is probably commensurate with that of the victim. The offender probably functions normally in employment and social circles and may or may not have prior criminal experience. The crime scene reflects intelligence and pre-meditation.

The FBI's Violent Crime Apprehension Program (VICAP), which facilitates communication and coordination between law enforcement agencies that investigate, track, and apprehend violent serial offenders, concluded that:

> The totality of the crime scene analysis indicates that the offender was well-organized in the preparation and execution of the crime. This was evidenced by the assailant's apparent familiarity with the victim's habits and neighborhood, the fact that the restraining device and weapon were brought to the scene in anticipation of victim confrontation, and the removal of the weapon from the residence.
>
> Additionally, the offender wore gloves resulting in a lack of fingerprints and other trace evidence. When coupled with the target, selected search of the residence for particular items of value, these characteristics point to the highly organized nature of this offense … The low-risk level exhibited by the victim suggests that she was more likely a victim of selection than a victim of opportunity.

Assistant District Attorney Richard Gordon argued: "A person who would break in to do a burglary is generally not there to do a homicide. They're there to steal things. So the fact that nothing was taken would seem to indicate that this was not the product of a burglary, that the homicide did not flow or result from a burglary."

"There didn't seem to be anything in the house that was disturbed … I mean, nothing was thrown around and—and it was significant because that seemed to indicate that it wasn't a robbery gone bad, that somebody breaking in to try to steal stuff hadn't tossed the house and—and then killed her," according to Assistant District Attorney Roberta Tepper.

And District Attorney Peter S. Gilchrist: "It was certainly my understanding that there was no evidence of a robbery and I'm assuming that everybody else was of the same opinion. I think that was pretty clear."

Who Killed Kim Thomas?

"Maybe it's worth investigating the unknown, if only because the very feeling of not knowing is a painful one."
~*Krzysztof Kieślowski*

The case captivated the city for weeks after it occurred, in 1994 when Edward was arrested, and again in 1995 when *The Charlotte Observer* ran a four-part series on the crime and its investigation. Although the case remains open, legal proceedings assert that the killer is almost surely one of two men: Marion Gales, one of several African-American handymen who at the time wound their way from the nearby low-income neighborhood of Grier Heights to Thomas' primarily white, middle-class subdivision, or her husband, Friedland … no clear answer has surfaced as to the question of guilt. Circumstantial evidence surrounds both suspects, but not enough to convict either one … No physical evidence links either man to the crime. Of four latent fingerprints found on the scene, only one was suitable for testing, and it didn't match any suspects or emergency personnel. The

> handcuffs were free of fingerprints. A cigarette butt at the scene didn't have enough saliva on it for DNA testing ... A stain in Friedland's car was human blood Type A, which was Kim's. However, it was too small to be tested accurately [for DNA]. Luminol testing for blood in the master bathroom sink was inconclusive.
>
> [Lewis, Cynthia. "Either/Or." *Charlotte Magazine*, May 31, 2006]

Marion Gales, who was initially investigated as a key suspect in Kim's murder, was known to have burglarized homes on Thomas' street. Gales was addicted to drugs, and a witness claimed to have seen him in the vicinity on the morning of the murder. In the weeks prior to her murder, Gales had also done odd jobs for Kim around their home. He was identified by Kim's friend, Jan Ellen Brown, as the man who cleaned her front stoop in June 1990.

Soon after Kim's murder, anonymous tips started coming in to Crime Stoppers, a national U.S. organization and network of local programs that work together to prevent and solve crimes, which claimed that Friedland was involved in an extramarital affair and alleged drug use. As a result, suspicion quickly shifted from Gales to Friedland. "The affair—with Bridgette David, a nurse with whom Friedland worked—was later confirmed to have been ongoing at the time of the murder, although it ceased soon after." (Lewis) He was later found to be involved in multiple affairs or casual sexual encounters during the course of his marriage to Kim.

In his initial interview, within hours of finding his wife's body, Friedland stated that he left home on the morning of July 27, 1990 at 7:45 a.m. and went to Presbyterian Hospital to make his rounds. At 10 a.m., he went to Charlotte Medical Center for an hour and returned to Presbyterian Hospital for two hours. Between 2 and 2:30 p.m., he went to his office on West Morehead Street and tried to call Kim. There was no answer.
He recalled staying at his office until 5:30 or 5:45 and then went back to Presbyterian Hospital until 8 p.m. He went back to Charlotte Medical Center and stayed until 8:30 p.m., and then went to the YMCA to work out until around 9:15 p.m. He then went to Mercy Hospital to the CCU and ICU. He last saw Chris Jones, a registered nurse, and left around 10 p.m., heading directly home.

Five days after Kim's death, August 1, 1990, investigators Hollingsworth and Buening asked Friedland to meet with them again to answer more questions.

> *Investigator:* Would she normally wear her rings? All the time? They weren't on her finger.

Friedland: The only time she might have taken them off would be to do some kind of heavy type of chemical cleaning work … but she didn't do much of that ...

Investigator: Friday morning, did she get up when you got up?

Friedland: She was a little bit slow, but by the time I was taking my shower, she already had the coffee going and she gave me a cup of coffee and I left the house with a cup of coffee … (The baby) was out of the crib. He was walking around.

Investigator: Would she normally go back to bed after you leave for work or - ?

Friedland: No, she might have. I had advised her on occasion to do that and I think it wouldn't have been out of her routine to say, 'all's quiet, (the baby's) gone down, I'll just sleep a little while longer.' That wouldn't be unheard of … He will usually be up until about 9 or 9:30 and then he will go back to sleep.

Investigator: Whenever he goes back down, then it wouldn't be unusual for Kim to lay back down and catch a little bit more sleep?

Friedland: Yes, if she was tired that morning, she might have laid down for a while.

Investigator: Did Kim normally sleep with ear plugs?

Friedland: Usually. She could hear the baby even with them in.

Investigator: Did Kim keep the alarm on when she was home?

Friedland: Kim always turned the alarm off when we got up. It wouldn't surprise me if she kept it off until night. Whenever I got home late at night, the alarm was on.

Investigator: We received a call, an anonymous call, from an individual who stated that you have a girlfriend who you've had for a long time. You're having an affair for a long time with a nurse and they gave the young lady's name. Said that both of you are married and are trying to get out of their marriages ... The young lady's name is Bridgette. You know the young lady named Bridgette?

Friedland: Yes, I do and what I'm going to need to do—again this is strictly confidential. I want to cooperate with you fully, you know. I'll talk to you in any kind of detail you want . . .

Investigator: Is there any truth to the fact that you were having an affair with another woman?

Friedland: I can't make any comment. As I said, I don't want you to interpret that to mean I am going to be …

Investigator: No, because you've been very cooperative. It's just some information that we need to verify… We might have to follow up …

Friedland: No, I'm perfectly willing, you know …

Investigator: We're not going to contact anybody else's spouse. By getting information from you, it makes it a lot simpler for us.

Friedland: I agree with what you're saying. My cooperation with you, it's going to be total and absolute. When there's a tragedy is that there is all kinds of … least of which there's the family, there's a child. I've been prepared for that since the moment and frankly I would have been a little bothered—I would have been a little bothered if this didn't come out. I'm not going to make any further comments … but you know … as I said, I will tell you everything.

Investigator: So what's Bridgette's last name?

Friedland: It's Bridgette David.

Investigator: Which hospital does she work at? The only stuff we can find out—it's easier …

Friedland: I know you can find it out. I know you can find it out, and I am willing to call my attorney now and have him come.

It doesn't matter to me. Okay.

Not because I don't want to be truthful with you. But you know it doesn't … people have told me that ever happens when you go in and talk to your attorney, talk to the police, you have your attorney. I realize I'm not under arrest and my life has been completely turned into a nightmare.

The police didn't prevent the murder but now everyone is going to be investigating my personal life and that is going to suffer. I was prepared for this. I don't expect you to disbelieve or believe any statement I make, but this is obviously a nightmare to me. And anything personal about me is just additional pain to me as just coincidental but nevertheless is something that can cause additional pain.

Friedland met with investigators two days later, Friday, August 3, 1990. This time, he brought his attorney Michael Scofield.

They asked him about possible threats, about the babysitter [Sara Briggs] who Kim had recently fired, whether Kim usually locked the door during the day time, and whether he locked the door when he left that morning. He said no to all those questions. They asked whether it was unlocked when he returned. Friedland said he put the key in, but didn't recall whether it was locked. They also asked him again about whether Kim had ever gotten out of bed that Friday morning.

Friedland responded:

> Before Kim even got up that morning … I was wearing that dark blue suit; that's a winter suit …
>
> At this point, as you can imagine having been through this story a zillion times, whether I'm recalling my previous stories, the original version, I mean I would have to trust my recollection of that—I was under incredible stress at the time. The statement that [I] originally gave is probably as accurate as I can give you now, but these additional details I didn't mention in the original statement like the fact that I had made this phone call to the Charlotte Memorial Hospital about this Mr. Wheeler and that I would have spent a little

> time in that den area loading up my pockets because I had to go downstairs that very morning because I've been so busy that I have been literally running out of clothes …
>
> You know again I thought—I mean I was re-creating for you my day, but obviously I mean there are inaccuracies there in the sense that now I'm telling you that that didn't even cross my mind. If I didn't tell you in the original statement that I went downstairs and got a dark blue suit. Yeah. Okay. That sort of thing. So therefore if I miss that you know.
>
> *Investigators:* ... when you left that particular day, do you know whether you locked the door?
>
> *Friedland:* No, I would not, to my knowledge. I would not take the key. If indeed she was up and said goodbye to me, which I originally recall. I lock the door if she is not awake … If she is awake, I don't leave an unlocked door. If she is awake, then I close the door and the locking decision is hers.

Investigators ask Friedland whether when he left for work that morning, he had to unlock the front door.

> *Friedland:* When I left for work, did I have to unlock the door? I mean, I would say yes to that just because—unless Rags the dog had

> been let out recently beforehand because he gets let out sometimes through that morning ritual. Rags has to run outside. That's another little detail. So the door is opening and closing at different times before I leave.

Among other things during the inquiry of Friedland on August 3, 1990, investigators also asked him questions about daily routines and habits, about the couple's adoption of Elliot.

> *Investigator:* Did you both want to adopt?
>
> *Friedland:* Kim was the activist in the adoption but I didn't object to it. It seemed very reasonable to me.
>
> *Investigator:* Do you love your child?
>
> *Friedland:* Immensely.
>
> *Investigator:* Do you want your child?
>
> *Friedland:* Absolutely. I mean that's one of the things that breaks my heart about this whole ordeal … I'm not the most expressive guy in the world and I was busy being a workaholic, but my responsibility to that child is absolutely zero difference whether he's an adopted or biological child …

Elizabeth Leland in her article "Could Her Husband Have Killed Her?" posits, "Investigators figured because Kim was wearing ear plugs, she hadn't got up. And if she hadn't got up, then Friedland is lying when he says she made him coffee and waved goodbye."

Investigators asked about Friedland's routine at the YMCA.

> *Friedland:* Chin-ups and sit-ups.
>
> *Investigator:* When you work out, do you wear anything on your hands?
>
> *Friedland:* Yes. I wear some gardener's gloves.
>
> *Investigator:* As we said to you—in the past—as we said to you before we started, no one's been eliminated.
>
> Did you kill your wife?
>
> *Friedland:* Absolutely not.

["Could Her Husband Have Killed Her?" | *The Charlotte Observer*, July 31, 1995, Elizabeth Leland]

Following the interview on August 3, Friedland refused to be interviewed by investigators without his attorney. When Investigator Booth called to ask Friedland for another interview, he refused and told Booth to "solve the goddamn crime." Several months later, police received a statement from Friedland's attorney:

> As you know, Dr. Friedland was exhaustively interviewed on a number of occasions by members of the police in the aftermath of his wife's death. The details of the scene and of his wife's appearance when he found her dead were related accurately at a time when those matters were fresh in his mind. Other intimate details of Kim's and his personal life were also discussed. In all, Dr. Friedland probably spent six or seven hours emptying his mind of information in response to the officers' inquiries. As you might imagine, it is very painful for Dr. Friedland to focus on these matters. If there is anything to add that would be helpful to the investigators, of course, Dr. Friedland is eager to provide whatever information you need. Since he has told you everything, however, further personal interviews would only be painful to him without serving any real purpose.

On August 22, 1990, Friedland spoke to the media for the first time, asking the public to come forward with information about the case. And on October 9, 1990, Friedland announced a private $25,000 reward fund started by Thomas' family and friends, the Kim Thomas Reward Fund. Ten days later, Friedland says that police had told him he was a suspect.

On June 25, 1991, Kim's parents, Lou and Helen, and her sisters, Joyce and Lynn, met with Charlotte police to issue another public plea for more information.

Friedland is Charged with the Murder of Kim Thomas

On Monday, July 11, 1994, Friedland was arrested and charged with the first-degree murder of his wife, Kim Thomas. The police were waiting for him at his office and made the arrest in the parking lot as he was getting out of his car. Friedland was held for three days and nights before his first court appearance, where the judge set the bond at $300,000. He put up his house and office as collateral.

The police had no hard evidence against Edward, but they had a theory—that he killed Kim because he didn't want to forfeit half his money and medical practice in a divorce. Then in 1993 investigator Walter Bowling found a pathologist in New York who would testify it was more likely Kim died before 7:30 a.m., before Edward left for work—a conclusion the medical examiner in Charlotte said he couldn't make.

Relying on the pathologist's testimony, Assistant District Attorney Richard Gordon took the case to the grand jury and in July 1994 Edward was charged.

["Case Against Friedland Unravels" | *The Charlotte Observer*, Elizabeth Leland, August 2, 1995]

The charges against Friedland were dropped on March 28, 1995, when Dr. Baden's key testimony regarding Kim's time of death was ruled inadmissible. The judge ruled that he would be allowed to testify about the approximate time Kim Thomas was slashed to death, but he wasn't permitted to tell jurors it was medically or scientifically certain that she died before Friedland left home July 27, 1990.

The judge ruled that Baden had to base his testimony on scientific factors alone and not be allowed to pinpoint a time of death or explain the anecdotal evidence that helped him form an opinion—which is something that medical examiners typically do.

The prosecutor, Assistant District Attorney Richard Gordon, said the decision to drop the charges against Friedland was based on this crucial ruling that would have kept Dr. Baden from telling jurors that Thomas "most likely" was killed approximately 30 minutes before Friedland told police he left for work.

In response to the charges being dropped, Friedland was quoted in an interview as saying: "There was justice done today." He continued to deny any involvement in Kim's death. "The evidence has never been there, and it never will be there because I had nothing to do with Kim's death. I am innocent."

Kim's father, Louis, in an interview, said Friedland is

> lucky to live in a country where the legal system has such a high standard for proof beyond a reasonable doubt … What happened today means Dr. Friedland is relieved of all charges right now, but that still leaves things open … I'll quote Yogi Berra: It's not over till it's over.
>
> ["Friedland Murder Charge Dropped" | *The Charlotte Observer*, March 29, 1995, Kathleen McClain, Mary Elizabeth Deangelis]

Friedland Files Wrongful Death Suit Against Marion Gales

In 1996, Friedland filed a wrongful death lawsuit in civil court against Marion Gales. Cynthia Lewis explains:

> The standard of proof for a civil suit is less stringent than that for a criminal case—a preponderance of evidence in the first instance, beyond a reasonable doubt in the second.
>
> It's a civil lawsuit, similar to the wrongful death suit filed against O.J. Simpson by the families of Nicole Brown Simpson and Ronald Goldman. That means the penalty is one of money, not prison. But unlike Simpson, Gales has no money. What Friedland wants is a legal finding that Gales is responsible for the murder.

In the March 30, 1996 *Charlotte Observer* article "MD Accuses Inmate Of Killing Wife," Elizabeth Leland writes:

> Ever since police targeted Dr. Edward Friedland as a suspect in his wife's murder in 1990, he's known the only way to show he didn't kill Kim Thomas was to prove someone else did.
>
> He's now trying to do just that.
>
> …Friedland filed a wrongful-death lawsuit against Marion Anthony Gales, a handyman serving 24 years in prison for first-degree burglary and breaking and entering. The suit claims that on July 27, 1990, Gales entered the unlocked Friedland-Thomas house and cut Thomas' throat.
>
> Friedland asks for an unspecified amount of money in damages, but his suit isn't about money. Gales doesn't have any.
>
> It's about redemption.
>
> Friedland is a branded man. A grand jury indicted him on a charge of murder in 1994, four years after Thomas was killed in their Churchill Road home. Even though prosecutors dropped the charge in March 1995, Friedland hasn't found a job as a kidney specialist. To rebuild his life, to regain his

standing in the medical community, he must prove someone else killed Thomas.
That's the ultimate goal of his suit: a legal finding that Gales is responsible for her murder.

'We have waited a year since the charges were dismissed,' said attorney David Rudolf of Chapel Hill, speaking on Friedland's behalf. 'We have asked police repeatedly about progress in their investigation. We're at the point now where we feel like we need to put forward the evidence that has been gathered in an effort to help Dr. Friedland put his life back together.'

'This is the final piece in trying to put some closure on the odyssey he's been put through for the last six years.'

In the opening statement in the Friedland v. Gales case, attorney Rudolf said:

'Marion Gales was out on the street. He was out on the street looking for crack cocaine. And he was looking for money to buy crack cocaine.'

In his closing statement, Rudolf argues:

'Now, by the summer of 1990, the collision course was set. Marion Anthony Gales was

> using crack cocaine, breaking into houses to trade for drugs.'

The jury agreed with Rudolf's argument and awarded Friedland $8.6 million in damages when they decided Kim Thomas was killed by Marion Gales, who was already in prison, and couldn't afford to pay his attorneys.

In *The Charlotte Observer* article, "Jury Blames Gales - Verdict A Step Toward Truth, Doctor Says" on October 4, 1997, the authors report:

> The wrongful-death case lasted nearly a month. It took jurors 5-1/2 hours over two days to reach a conclusion. Among the most compelling evidence, one juror said: testimony from a fellow inmate that while in prison Gales confessed to the killing.
>
> Though Gales' attorneys painted inmate Jeffrey Carter as a known liar, he testified to details that were confirmed by other witnesses. Carter said Gales sat on the slate steps in Thomas' house near her body and tossed his shoes away while fleeing. There were three steps a few feet from Thomas' body; and Gales showed up at his sister's house the morning of the killing wearing no shoes.
>
> 'I, like every other juror in the jury box, felt in 1990 like Friedland had something to do with it, but that probably changed during the

course of the trial,' said one juror, who asked not to be identified.
'Quite frankly, neither the plaintiff nor the defendant was stellar in his own way. But just because a guy doesn't have a good marriage doesn't mean he's going to kill his wife. There was opportunity and motive on the part of Gales.'

Juror Jerry Creel, 62, said it became obvious to the jurors that the police made mistakes in their case against Friedland.

'It was just evident that they were not pursuing evidence presented to them. It seemed that they were after Mr. Friedland so strongly that they ignored evidence,' Creel said.

Friedland's character wasn't beyond reproach, he said. 'He admitted some stuff there on the stand that I myself now would not use him as a doctor. But I don't think he killed his wife. I don't know that Marion Gales did it, but I feel it was more likely that he did it than he did not.'

In this civil case, jurors needed only to decide it was more likely than not that Gales did the killing. In a criminal trial, jurors would have to decide if a person is guilty beyond all reasonable doubt.

Therefore, circumstantial evidence prevailed, including such details as: Gales owned handcuffs; he carried a knife; he owned shoes similar to those that left prints at the scene; he was seen that morning on Churchill Road; and his brother-in-law said he appeared that day to have blood on his clothes.

There was not a scrap of physical evidence connecting Gales to the scene. That's inconsistent with other burglaries Gales committed in which he left all kinds of evidence, his attorneys said.

'There were no fingerprints,' said Sharon Jumper, who often led Gales' defense. 'He didn't become a smart criminal overnight. If you believe some of the testimony in evidence, he left no trace. Nothing.'

Gales denied any involvement in the murder and his attorneys quickly filed an appeal. Frank Creft, one of four *pro bono* attorneys who defended Gales, said: 'We still believe Mr. Gales did not commit the offense … This is an issue of liability, and he's not guilty.'

In response to the ruling, Friedland said:

'I feel we've made an important step forward to set the record straight and get the truth out

> … We need to make sure that there is complete justice for Kim and a complete understanding of what happened in this investigation … This is certainly not the end of anything.'

Following the ruling in the Gales case, in 1997, Friedland brought another suit against the City of Charlotte and four police officers, claiming malicious prosecution. Attorney David Rudolf said that Friedland's victory in the wrongful-death case in civil court proves the police screwed up.

Kim's family did not believe Gales was responsible for her murder. Louis Thomas said that the Friedland vs. Gales trial was not about who killed Thomas. It was about Friedland vs. Gales. He believed Friedland's suit against the city would be more important:

> 'It showed that preparation and money will win,' he said. 'I really didn't understand this method of Dr. Friedland trying to prove he was innocent in the death of my daughter by accusing someone else … Logic tells you they're going to be better prepared than the volunteer lawyers who got into the trial at the eleventh hour,' he said. 'I hope somewhere down the line that we'll find out who killed Kim Thomas.'

Speaking to a reporter about the Gales trial, Lynn Thomas said: "It's like an atomic bomb that goes off," she said. "All you can do is try to pick up the pieces."

> This bomb shattered the lives of three families, ended the life of one young mother, and despite the verdict there will always be questions about who lit the fuse. Still the families will deal with the pain and rebuild their lives. Somehow it will get easier as the years roll by. And it may turn out that the only person to ever receive a final judgment in the Kim Thomas case is Kim Thomas. She was sentenced to death. And no matter how many years go by, she will be 32 forever.
>
> ["Families Able To Heal, But Victims Aren't" | *The Charlotte Observer*, October 4, 1997, Tommy Tomlinson]

A trial judge initially overturned the verdict of the civil suit against Gales on the technicality that the suit was brought outside the statute of limitations; however, the North Carolina Court of Appeals subsequently upheld it.

Friedland v. City of Charlotte

In 1997, Friedland brought another civil lawsuit—this time for malicious prosecution—against the City of Charlotte and the four individual investigators. That lawsuit was dropped five years later after being dismissed as a summary judgment motion six times by three state and three federal courts. [A summary judgment is a judgment entered by a court for one party against another party without a full trial.]

In his state-court complaint filed June 2, 1997, plaintiff [Edward Friedland] sued the City of Charlotte and four of its police officers for malicious prosecution, infliction of emotional distress, and violation of the state constitution. Although the plaintiff could have brought these Section 1983 claims in state court under the doctrine of concurrent jurisdiction, he chose, instead, to proceed in both courts. In the state action, plaintiff alleged that police failed to investigate Ms. Thomas' murder properly and failed to provide the exculpatory evidence [Evidence favorable to the defendant in a criminal trial that exonerates or tends to exonerate the defendant of guilt], discussed supra [above], to the district attorney prior to indictment. It was the plaintiff's contention that those failures caused the district attorney to obtain a grand jury indictment of him without probable cause and in violation of his state due-process rights [guarantee that a person has the right to the fair application of the law before they can be imprisoned, executed, or have their property seized].

About the case, Cynthia Lewis explains:

> Friedland and his lawyers contended that inexperienced detectives had botched the investigation of the crime scene. Most of the investigators assigned to the case were indeed relatively new, and they made some obvious mistakes, such as using luminol testing for blood before luma-lite testing for hair and fiber, which luminol can disperse. Still, Friedland's own expert on crime scene processing testified during his prosecution that Charlotte police had done 'a fairly good job of documenting this crime scene,' and Friedland's attorneys conceded that the police did an 'immediate and thorough' job, and that their efforts were 'intensive.'
>
> Despite a scarcity of physical evidence—or perhaps because of it—every detail of the crime scene became a point of contention. Did the victim's blood, found in a secluded office in her home, come from her open wounds while she was still alive or from the killer's bloody gloves, clothing, or weapon? Was the killer looking for

something in particular as he riffled through papers in the office, replacing them neatly and closing the drawers, or was he deliberately misleading investigators as to his motive? Was the extreme violence of the murder—described by nearly everyone but Friedland's attorneys as "overkill"—a sign of intimacy between the victim and her attacker—or of a drug-induced frenzy? … Was the dog Rags passive and friendly or aggressive and likely to bark at an intruder?

[Lewis, Cynthia. "Either/Or." *Charlotte Magazine*, May 31, 2006
https://www.charlottemagazine.com/either-or/]

[For more, see Defense Overview and Excerpts from Friedland v. City of Charlotte on page 232.]

In Memoriam, Kim's Life & Remembrances

Kim's Life: A Timeline

1958

June 8: Kim Ann Thomas is born to Helen and Louis Thomas in Beth Israel Hospital in Newark, NJ.

1976

Kim graduates from Westfield Senior High School. Begins college at University of Rochester.

1979

Kim meets Edward Friedland at the University of Rochester.

1980

Kim graduates from University of Rochester with a bachelor of science in psychology and starts her master's program in Music at Eastman School of Music.

1981

Kim receives her master's degree from University of Rochester.

Friedland graduates from University of Rochester School of Dentistry and Medicine. They move to NYC where Friedland completes his internship at Mount Sinai Beth Israel. Kim works at WNYC.

1982

Kim and Friedland get engaged. Kim breaks off the engagement. Friedland moves to Miami, FL for his Fellowship and Residency in Nephrology at Jackson Memorial Hospital.

1983

Kim and Friedland get re-engaged and she moves to Miami.

1984

Kim and Friedland are married in NJ on April 15 and take a three-week honeymoon to Italy. Kim becomes a Financial News Network (FNN) anchor in Miami.

1985

Kim becomes a stock broker with Merrill Lynch.

1986

Kim and Friedland move to Charlotte, NC. Friedland becomes the medical director of Charlotte Nephrology Dialysis Centers.

1987

Kim and Friedland purchase their first and only home at 3853 Churchill Road in Charlotte.

1988

Kim tries twice to get pregnant through GIFT (precursor to IVF). Eventually, they decide to adopt.

Kim writes a book with Nancy Verruto, *A Charlotte Child.*

1989

Kim and Friedland adopt Elliot Roy Friedland. Elliot is born on September 8 in Houston, TX. Kim acts as the birth coach for Elliot's biological mother. She stays in Houston until all legal issues are resolved. Kim's parents join her for the two weeks she needs to remain in Houston to sort through the legal adoption papers for North Carolina's first independent adoption. Kim returns to Charlotte with Elliot on September 20. Friedland's office throws them a baby shower on September 21. Hurricane Hugo hits Charlotte on the morning of September 22. Much of their property is destroyed and they are without power for two weeks (with a newborn!).

1990

July 20: Kim, Friedland, and Elliot go to Blowing Rock, NC, for a weekend family vacation. July 26: Kim records on video Friedland carrying a bird that fell through the chimney out to the deck. It ends at 8:46 p.m.—the last moment she is known to be alive.

July 27: Kim is found by Friedland, murdered, in her home at 9:54 p.m. and pronounced dead at 10:06 p.m.

July 29: Kim's memorial service was held at Harry & Bryant Funeral Home, Charlotte, NC.

A Brief Life, Lived to the Fullest

"Memories of our lives, of our works and our deeds will continue in others."
~*Rosa Parks*

Kim was born on June 8, 1958, at Beth Israel Hospital in Newark, NJ, the third daughter of Helen and Louis Thomas. Friends and family describe her as larger than life, smart, passionate, if not impetuous. Her sister Lynn says she was good at everything she did from a young age, whether it was school or sports or music. Kim played both the clarinet and piano, and both teachers would remark at how naturally gifted she was.

When Lynn called her piano teacher, Mr. Somers, to tell him of Kim's murder, he was shocked. "How? When? Why?" He said that she was his favorite and most talented student. Somers relayed that he enjoyed teaching her immensely and said if she had had the discipline to practice, she could have been a concert pianist. She also played the clarinet. Her clarinet teacher, Mr. Pappas, each week would say how much she improved from the previous week and complimented her on her practicing. She rarely, if ever, practiced.

Kim met her first best friend Philip Rudder when he was 5 and she was 6. They were neighbors. They had signals they would send to each other when they were home by flicking their bedroom lights on and off. There were different signals for when they wanted to talk on the phone, meet outside, when it was time to come over for dinner, or hang out on the roof, or play football. The two of them shared the ups and downs of growing up and teenage life, and more. Philip has said: "Kim was my best friend, and no one would ever come close."

"To me, as one of her younger cousins, Kim Thomas seemed like most likely to conquer the world," Jackie Orr remembers.

> She was energetic, smart, funny, and beautiful—both inside and out. People were drawn to her positive energy and bubbly personality. She radiated an inner warmth, making each person feel special. Some of my earliest and fondest memories of Kim were when she used to sing to me as a small child and play the guitar or the piano. One favorite song she used to sing to me was, 'Wynken, Blynken, and Nod.' It is such a special memory, when I had my own kids, I found the poem and used to read it to them and think of her.

Another of Jackie's favorite memories of her older cousin, Kim:

> Every Thanksgiving, after our big family dinner, we had a long-standing tradition—all of our parents stayed home and played cards, and the cousins (old and young) all went out together, most often to the movies. One year, it was snowing, and our older cousins convinced my parents and the other aunts and uncles it would be totally fine. We all packed into the car … definitely more than would be permitted by today's standards, and Kim drove safely to the movies. Then, in the parking lot, she went crazy—doing donut after donut in the snow, sliding the car everywhere, and spinning away! Everyone was screaming and laughing. The back car door even flew open mid-donut—terrifying and thrilling all at once. Totally Kim. Calm and peaceful one minute and crazy the next.

"She was the world to me," explained her cousin Melissa Kassel. Growing up together and the same age, Kim and Melissa were extremely close. "She was my buddy and playmate from the time we were very young." Their families often vacationed together and their parents went out together every Saturday evening for 30 years—(which is sometimes when the duo got themselves into trouble).

Melissa explains,

> From around age 3 to 19 or 20, Kim was my best friend. We grew up in the same town. I

> remember riding to nursery school together. We went on family vacations together. From seventh grade through high school, I spent almost every Saturday night at the Thomas home with her. I would ride my bike over on Saturday morning and leave on Sunday morning. There are so many years and memories with Kim that it's hard to break it down.
>
> Torturing Lynn, hitchhiking through NJ, smoking a lot of pot, drinking our parents' alcohol when they were out to dinner—so many memories. I can close my eyes now and I can see her so clearly, down to the shape of her fingernails.

When they were kids, Kim lied to Melissa and told her that she was on the children's television show Romper Room. "I was very jealous of her," Melissa explains with a laugh, "until I found out that it wasn't true."

On one family vacation, a cruise, when they were around 11 years old, the two girls wandered around the ship and pretended they were British, with affected accents and all. "We met some nuns who we befriended and tried to help during the cruise," Melissa recalls. As they were getting off the ship at the end of the cruise with their families, they ran into the nuns who exclaimed, "Oh look, it's those nice British girls who helped us!"

On another family vacation at the Mount Washington Hotel when they were around 12 or 13 years old, the two girls decided that they needed to feed the elevator operators so they would bring their food from dinner to serve to them.

> We collected blackberries and made jam on that trip. We spent the afternoon squishing up blackberries and presented them to everyone at dinner. We were so excited. There was not a shy bone in her body. She was just able to be out there. She was a dynamo.
>
> We separated for a bit in our early 20s. We were so close, I think we needed to separate to gain our own identities. We were just starting to get back together soon before she died.

Since Kim's death, Melissa has written songs, including one titled "For Kim" and a poem about their childhood together. As a singer, Melissa explains that early in her career she explored a lot of Avant Garde music "probably to scream the pain [of Kim's murder] out of me." She explains further:

> I think part of me was inspired by her to be who I needed to be—a musician and vocalist. As kids, Kim would play the piano and I would sing and she would tell me how good I was, always encouraging me. She was a jack of all trades and wandered through a lot of things very well.

I never thought she wasn't going to be in my life. I thought that we would grow old together. And I never thought I wouldn't have the chance to have her as my best friend again. I actually never wanted to have kids until after she was murdered. After that, I felt this intense need to have more sparks of life and bring more joy into the world. And I decided I wanted to be a parent.

Listen to Melissa sing her song "For Kim"

Kim's Life in Photos

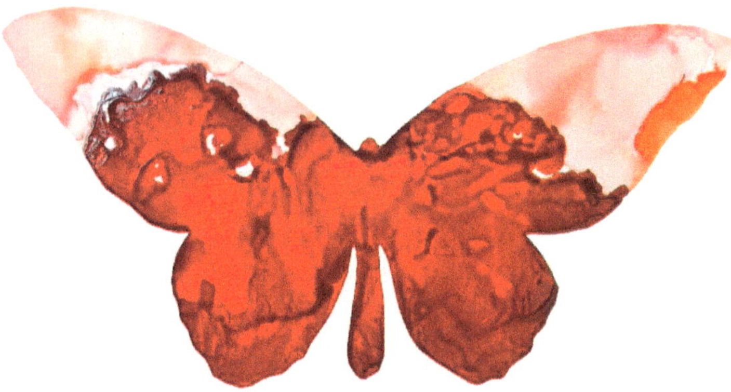

Kim Thomas, c.1960

Thomas Sisters, Lynn, Kim, Joyce, c. 1960

Sisters visiting Santa, c. 1962

Lynn & Kim, c. 1963

Thomas Sisters, c. 1966

Kim, only girl on the football team, c. 1968

Kim's sixth grade class, NJ, c. 1970

Kim on piano, c. 1971

Kim, c. 1973

Kim and Lynn, 1974

University of Rochester Graduation, 1980

University of Rochester Graduation, 1980

University of Rochester Graduation, 1980

Kim, c. 1980

Engagement Party, 1982

Friend's wedding, c. 1984

Lynn and Kim, 1984

Kim and Lynn, 1984

Wedding photo, 1984

Kim, Boston, c. 1985

Martinique, 1986

Kim and Rags, Winter 1987

Kim and Rags, Winter 1987

Louis, Kim, Helen Thomas, 1988

Kim, Christmas, c. 1988

New Year's Eve, Spain, 1988

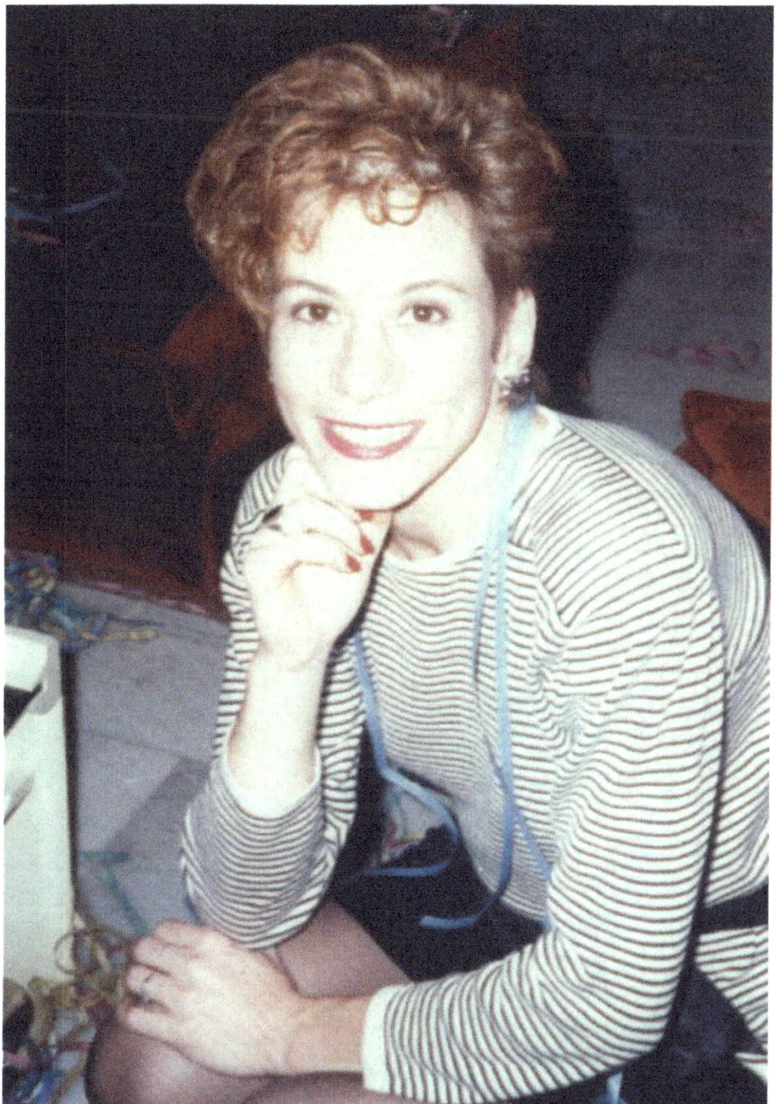

New Year's Eve, Spain, 1988

Kim, 1988

Kim, Churchill Rd., Charlotte 1988

Kim, Churchill Rd., Charlotte 1988

A Charlotte Child book cover

Kim and Elliot, Fall 1989

Kim and Elliot, Fall 1989

Kim, Elliot, and Lynn, baby shower, 1989

Kim and Elliot, Fall 1989

Pumpkin, Elliot & Rags, Charlotte, Fall 1989

Kim and Elliot, 1990

Edward, Kim, and Elliot, 1990

Adulthood and Marriage

"sweet girl,
it wasn't that you weren't enough,
it's your energy … it asks
others to rise up,
and not everyone is willing to go where they
would grow"

~*butterflies rising*

Kim attended The University of Rochester, where she worked on her bachelor's degree in psychology. She was a cocktail waitress with her friend Judy Perlman at the Elmwood Inn near campus, where she first waited on and met Edward Friedland in 1979. Judy waited on Edward first. He had ordered a martini. She disliked him immediately, and said to her co-workers: "I don't want to go back and deal with that guy … anyone else can." Kim said she would wait on him, and friends recall that Kim liked Friedland from the start.

Sure, she wrote in her journal, there were some things about him she disliked. She hated the way his lips cracked when they got dry and his face became rough when he needed a shave.

But Ed was brilliant. He graduated from high school in New York City at age 16, from Columbia University at 20. Kim admired his discipline and focus, the fact that he wanted to be the best doctor possible. He didn't care what people thought of him, and she found that refreshing. Best of all, he made her laugh. Edward dealt with stress by making a joke of it.

["Who Killed Kim Thomas?" | *The Charlotte Observer*, Elizabeth Leland, July 30, 1995]

Kim's journal was very important and personal to her. She followed the *intensive journal method*, "a psychotherapeutic technique largely developed in 1966 at Drew University and popularized by Ira Progoff (1921–1998). It consists of a series of writing exercises using loose leaf notebook paper in a simple ring binder, divided into sections to help in accessing various areas of the writer's life. These include a dialogue section for the personification of things, a 'depth dimension' to aid in accessing the subconscious and other places for recording remembrances and meditations."

> [Note: Please bear in mind that these are her private thoughts and explorations that Kim likely never expected anyone to read. However, we believe they are important to getting to the core of who Kim was and in telling the story of her life.]

She worked and studied a year in the sound department at the Eastman School of Music and obtained a master's degree in music. When Friedland finished medical school, they moved to New York City. During her time there, she worked as a voice-over artist with WNYC. According to her journal, they had lots of ups and downs. During one of the good times in 1982, they were walking down Second Avenue and Friedland proposed to her. Kim wrote in her journal:

> The park, the orange Dart, and Eddie saying "there comes a time in a man's life"... Dark night - after a barbecue, terrace overlooking Southern Manhattan.
>
> "Will you marry me?" Ed asked.
>
> Silence.
>
> *Edward:* "Yes? No?" he asked again. "Yes? No?"
>
> *Kim:* "Well, I guess so."
>
> *Edward:* "You guess so? It's either Yes or No."
>
> *Kim:* "Yes."

They were engaged in 1982, but a few months later, Kim broke off the engagement. Her journal entries during that time show her ambivalence:

February 13, 1982
Eddie says that we are shattered. We love each other but we can't live with each other. We enjoy and like each other but we get on each other's nerves. Movement to this point has been (up and down)—hopes are that we can marry someday—disappoints are that we have to separate in May and fear is that we will never see each other again.

Sadness—I feel sad when reading this statement.

It was a time when I wanted to be a mother and wife but still was a young woman when the romance of the moment and tribulation of my inner conflict peaked: As I was saying "YES," my thoughts screamed "NO." The desire to buy an engagement ring and thoughts of non-engagement if no ring was bought. The ring was beautiful—it still brings tears to my eyes.

Scared stiff the evening before the ring was to be delivered; crying to my folks—Mom saying that I wanted it and Dad saying I've got time.

The ring—Eddie, Oh was I right in giving it back to him?

Yes, I have little conflict now.

But in these dis-engaged days we sort of sit around wondering why we're together and scared to break apart. But Eddie is going to Florida in May. I will be on my own—scared, lonely. And time will tell between us whether we have the stuff for a lasting relationship or not. The engagement is off, the ring in a safe deposit box—our life together shaky.

It is a moment not too long ago—not the immediate past, but close to my present. Constant thinking and re-thinking of my relationship with him.

February 26, 1982
We cannot transmit our feelings very well therefore we misunderstand each other's words, thoughts, expressions.

Friedland decided to leave New York for Miami for his residency. He was accepted at Jackson Memorial Hospital. He asked Kim to come with him, but she declined at that time. That summer, 1982, Kim lived with her parents. She missed Friedland and talked with him a lot by telephone. She enjoyed being free, not committed, not hurting herself or anyone else. She briefly fell for another man.

But in the spring of 1983, things with Friedland started to rekindle. They talked about her joining him in Miami—to see if they could make it work. "I'm willing to give Miami and Eddie a shot," she wrote in her journal on April 15, 1983. "But I wish the stakes were more even. Even though I don't have rent or a job at the moment, I'm going to be leaving my family, my friends and my voice teacher."

She moved to Miami in late May. Three months later, they were engaged again.

> *September 22, 1983*
> It's good. I hope we have long, happy, fruitful lives together ... I think he will soon want the intimacy I crave now. Men and women have different needs at different times in their lives. Unfortunately they do not coincide. At least Eddie wants babies soon. I'll have my intimacy then.

Kim and Friedland married on April 15, 1984, before 250 guests at the Crystal Plaza, in New Jersey.

> *May 1984*
> Eddie and I have much happiness ... We have sadness, too. But most importantly, we have each other for our lives together and we can shape and mold a wonderful future.

In true Kim fashion, she talked her way into a newscaster's job at Financial News Network's Miami cable station. Lynn remembers:

> Kim called me the evening before her job interview. She asked me what she should wear. She had a great red dress she wanted to wear or some business suits. I told her I thought that a financial news network would look for an anchor person who dressed the part, which would be more conservative than flashy and colorful. She agreed, or so I thought. She called me after the interview and told me she got the job. She wore her red dress to the lunch interview, and she was offered the job. This is a perfect example of how Kim did Kim as only she could. If anyone else wore a red dress, that person would not have been offered the job.

She loved her new job and she was a natural on camera. Friends recall that Friedland was proud of his wife's accomplishments on FNN. If he was free when she was on (which was 5 minutes to the hour and 25 minutes past each hour), he would turn on the television to watch her, making sure to shush everyone around him.

Watch Kim's demo reel from FNN

She was a recognized minor celebrity in the Miami area. When Kim went to meet her parents at the airport when they arrived for a visit, a number of their fellow passengers remarked that they watched her on FNN. Lynn recalls that when she was visiting Kim in Miami that she was regularly recognized on the street as a celebrity. She anchored the show for a couple of years, but when the station switched to a Spanish format, she was out of a job.

Kim and her sisters grew up sitting with their father around the dinner table each evening listening to and discussing the stock reports. She already knew the basics about the stock market, so it made sense when she was looking for a new job to become a stockbroker. Kim started a training program with Merrill Lynch, but stayed for less than a year.

Lynn recalls that when she was visiting Kim in Miami, Kim lamented that she wanted to spend more time with her, but had to go to work the next day. Right then and there, in the Jacuzzi, she announced: "Well, you know what? I'm not really happy being a stockbroker anyway, so I think I'll quit tomorrow, then we'll have more time to spend together while you are here." Lynn responded, "I don't think Mom or Dad will be happy about that." Kim giggled and said, "Okay, fine, I'll wait a day." So she waited a day and she just quit.

She realized that she needed to be in a more creative environment than Wall Street would provide. She wanted to explore her philosophical and spiritual sides. She daydreamed of learning languages and regularly flying off to other countries, living with artists and soaking up their creativity—perhaps, even starting a small business.

Kim and Friedland talked about having a baby. But because of his work, he reminded her, he wouldn't be around much to help take on the responsibility. He told her that he wasn't sure they were stable enough to raise children. Kim told Friedland that he needed to see a shrink or that they should get counseling or split up.

Kim wanted a compassionate and sensitive man, aggressive and exciting, yet stable. Someone who adored her. Someone to woo her with flowers and perfume even after 10 years of marriage. A doer. A dreamer. A lover.

She thought Ed needed a woman who was … like he was, someone who could have a career and give him babies, who would be proud of her husband, the doctor. Ed thought their marriage had no future. It was true, Kim admitted in her journal in March 1986, they saw life differently. Maybe Ed was right, they should split up.

["Who Killed Kim Thomas?" | *The Charlotte Observer*, Elizabeth Leland, July 30, 1995]

They moved to Charlotte in 1986 where Friedland became the medical director of Mecklenburg Dialysis Centers.

***

For all of her searching for a career and path in life that would allow her to fully be herself, the main constant in her life, according to friends and family, was Kim's zest for life and the fierceness with which she loved her friends and family. She tried to help those around her to be the best they could and encouraged others to live life "big and authentically," recalls Lynn.

Nancy Verruto met Kim and Friedland when they were moving into the apartment complex where Nancy and her husband, Michael, lived in Charlotte. "Being nosy neighbors, we knocked on their door to introduce ourselves. Because her husband was busy building his practice, Kim and I spent a lot of time together and were instant friends. She pressed me into leaving my job as a stockbroker so that we could find a career that we would love and that we could do together. We threw around lots of ideas over many glasses of wine—like opening a store or starting an event planning business—but then we decided we would write a book."

"We were both feminists," Nancy explains.

> We read an article that doctors were giving women caesareans at an alarming rate and when it wasn't necessary and that got us thinking about babies and motherhood. There were so many babies being born in Charlotte at that time—so *A Charlotte Child* was born. It kind of felt like we birthed the book. It was a guide for pregnant women specific to Charlotte—a chronological guide and workbook—with topics ranging from how and where to buy the best crib to what questions to ask your obstetrician.

See more about *A Charlotte Child*

> We had sort of a sister bond and were just very comfortable with each other. We didn't need to talk. When not researching our next career move, we often would just sit quietly or watch TV at my house because I had a three-year-old daughter, who decided that Kim was

> her friend, not mine. She loved Kim and would have been very content to cut me out of the loop or go on lunch dates alone with Kim.

In Charlotte, she became very active in the community. Kim served on a task team for creating new policies for independent adoptions in the Mecklenburg County Department of Social Services and co-chaired the Southern Piedmont Adoptive Families of America. Kim was the leader of the Charlotte Chapter of the National Organization for Women.

[See *The Charlotte Observer* article about Kim's involvement with NOW on page 258].

Kim Merrill, who met Kim through NOW, reminisces:

> I loved her belief in possibilities and her refusal to think in terms of 'no' or 'it can't be done.' She seemed to make everyone who worked with her believe change and progress were possible. Her personality was infectious. You just wanted to be around her optimistic and 'can-do' energy.

Kim's sister Lynn recalls:

> Kim's life was never ordinary or boring or average. Nothing about Kim was insignificant. She lived life large, and loud when necessary, and was damn proud to do so. She spoke out against wrongs, took

stances where needed, marched in picket lines when necessary.

While she was in the process of adopting her son, Kim challenged the hospital's policy, which required a 48-hour waiting period for an adoptive mother to hold her child and won; she was able to hold her son, Elliot, in her hotel room within 24 hours of his birth.

Kim worked to change the laws in North Carolina to legalize independent adoptions. And she never, ever wavered in her shining, devoted love of her family and friends. If she had lived, Kim would've had a huge impact on the world—bettering life for others. I'm not sure how she would've done it, but I know she would've lived big.

Taken From Us

"Each man's life touches so many lives," says Clarence. "When he isn't around, he leaves an awful hole, doesn't he?"
~*It's a Wonderful Life*

It's an overwhelming shock when someone's life ends in such a violent way; the lasting effects can be felt for years—and across generations. It's these aftershocks and memories that can be most difficult over the long-term for family and friends, especially when there are so many unanswered questions.

There were the little quirky things about her personality and being that friends and family realize they still miss: the sound of Kim's voice, the very tone and cadence when she spoke, her scent, her laugh, the mischievous sparkle in her eyes. Though her years on Earth were brief, the seismic and colossal waves of Kim's life and death are still reverberating. "Kim was just a source of utter joy," explains her sister Lynn.

> She provided a lot of affirmation for me, which I didn't feel from many of my family members. She believed in me more than I believed in me, and she had this great way of giving feedback that was non-

> confrontational, which was sincere, and made me take it to heart. Kim was my best friend and soul sister. No one else will ever come close.

Kim made numerous recordings for friends and family members that now provide insights into who she was. She would detail her daily activities since their last correspondence and share new life milestones. She inquired about the minute details of their lives, wanting to know about absolutely everything.

In a tape recorded for her friend Sherry Picker at the end of May 1990, Kim talks about their approaching, shared birthday month of June and about the joy and inevitable exhaustion that baby Elliot had brought to her life. She continued to provide a thorough account of the quiet, but otherwise pleasant weekend she had just spent with her family. After which, she proclaimed that she had a new life philosophy that she was working on developing.

"Do you want to hear it?" she asks in the cassette as if she may receive a response from Sherry. "Okay, here it is," she continues:

> Life — each day — is like a piece of art and you need to take the time to do the things you do in it. Treat your day as if you were creating a painting ... you have to carefully select the colors for your palette. And you need to realize

> that each day has a beginning, a middle, and an end, and you should try to develop some rhythm to your day. So, try to live it in a full way and enjoy everything you're doing while you're doing it, cause you won't be doing it very long! Sometimes it really rings true and I can do it and sometimes I can't.

Kim lets out a quick, boisterous laugh and moves on to the next topic.

Listen to an excerpt from the recording

Sherry recalls:

> She was all about living life as art—start with a blank canvas, fill it with composition, color, paint the life that you want to. I was so excited when I would come home and see that I had received a cassette 'letter' from Kim. We would record messages and send them back and forth frequently. I believe she was someone who would've been a lifelong friend—surviving time and distance. I've

> known people in my life for longer, but they never had the impact she had on me.
>
> She taught me that people could have intimacy without physical intimacy. One time, she made me get the dictionary to look up the word. I knew how to spell the word, but that was about it. She was the first person to open me up. She taught me how to love.

Ellyn Silverman, who met Kim through an adoption support group, remembers the first time they met. Kim was gregarious and welcomed her with open arms, which was exactly what she needed after a difficult time going through in-vitro treatments and trying to navigate the adoption process. Kim was already going through the adoption process, and Kim helped Ellyn through the process, including writing and placing an ad for a birth mother and being there when their first adoption attempt fell through. The two became tight friends as they went through the adoption process. Ellyn explains, "It really bonds you—experiencing the ups and downs."

Ellyn's daughter was born in October of 1989, just six weeks after Elliot, and she says that Kim was there when Ellyn got off the airplane with her daughter to welcome them home and wrap her arms around them.

"She was just in the blossoming of the story of who she would become," says Ellyn.

> She had already done so much before, including helping people through the adoption process. People wouldn't have their children if it weren't for Kim. I wouldn't have my daughter—and now granddaughter—if it weren't for Kim Thomas.

She still cries when she talks about Kim.

> Her name has not left the people she touched. She has never left my being. Every year on the anniversary of her death, I light a candle. It's a definite trauma when something like this happens. Then to be traumatized by everything that happened around her murder and not having answers. You don't let go of a person who touches you so intimately.

A number of years ago, Ellyn visited Kim's grave and recalls saying, "I have no clue who you would've been, but I know I would've been amazed."

In a card with a print of Monet's "The Artist's Garden at Vétheuil" that Kim sent to Lynn, a few months prior to her murder, Kim writes:

> Ah well according to my new philosophy (well let's say formalized not new) may you walk slowly in a garden of flowers and for several minutes you absorb the odors, colors, textures, and sounds so deeply that you become part of the garden.

Even those who didn't know Kim sought association with her after her death. Tales of acquaintance with Kim were told far and wide around Charlotte—about how they had grown up with her, attended scouts or camp with her—even though she didn't grow up in the area.

A homicide detective who worked on the case attended the 10-year anniversary vigil and with tears told her family, "I only knew Kim in death, but 10 years after I die, there would not be this many people at my memorial service. She lived life fully every day and I am inspired to live my life more fully."

Robin Underwood, a friend from Charlotte, who with her boyfriend frequently socialized with Kim, Friedland, Nancy, and Michael, remembers one evening when their "gang of six" planned a murder mystery dinner at Kim's and Friedland's home.

> At the time, it was an ordinary thing to do, very much in vogue … the murder mystery dinner. I brought a murder mystery box for us to play. Dinner was delayed, Kim was microwaving potatoes, and Friedland was criticizing her cooking. I never imagined we would want to solve a real murder in that house.

Steve Schramm, a childhood friend, recalls:

> I met her in fifth grade, began conversing with her in eighth grade, and hung out with her intermittently in high school. She hung

out as 'one of the guys'—I presume as a moderator. She was comfortable in her own skin.

During the summer of 1977 or 1978, we started hanging out. She would watch me dive (springboard) at Mountainside pool, and I used to play piano for her. She had expressive, mischievous eyes, with a voice that was rhythmic with a wide range of tones. On her 17th birthday, I remember that I gave her a Greek-named Jade plant with goldfish flowers.

We exchanged letters throughout college. And while she was in SOHO and I was in Rutgers Medical School, I visited her a few times. We went canoeing and out to some South American jazz club near her apartment. I recall her mentioning some problems with Friedland like when they had broken up. I lost touch with Kim in 1984. I began my medical training in Columbia, SC, and began a Family Practice in Atlanta in 1987.

I had always longed to have a deep relationship with Kim, but I lacked the courage to pursue it. She was known fondly by my friends as: 'Yhom.' I was shy growing up and never talked so deeply about opinions and feelings until I met Kim. Kim had such a musical, lyrical voice that mesmerized me. She definitely had strong opinions, but was so engaging and such a good listener. We laughed together more than I have with any other woman.

I miss Kim very much, but I am also grateful for the thrilling, joyful moments she has given me. She made life better.

Many of us trudge through life looking for that 'right' person—someone who is supportive, mindful, credible, trustworthy, beautiful. In my adult life, I have not met someone as impactful or wonderful as Kim.

After hearing from her sister Lynn about Kim's later philosophy on life, it reinforced my memory of Kim being profound, inquisitive, colorful, and artistic. What I remember most is her playfulness, her vocal expressiveness, and her mischievous eyes. Sensible has a different meaning for Kim. She used all five senses and was SO observant. Kim had the unique combination of strong ideas, veracity, honesty, and independence, and yet openness to others.

Kim knows I love her. She lives on with me.

Steve's sister Laurie Schramm Levites remembers that she first became close to Kim in junior high school.

There were three couples in ninth grade at Roosevelt Junior High that had a long-term relationship for an entire year, which was a big deal for 15 year olds. We were all constantly together at friends' houses, parties, hanging out at the bleachers behind the school at Roosevelt, and swinging on the swings.

I remember a pool party specifically where Kim (who was pretty developed and looked cute in a bikini) had her photo taken [by the *Newark Evening News*] as she lounged by the pool at Mountainside Swim Club. The caption read something like, 'Handling the heat by the side of the pool.' In a teenager's mind that made her famous.

My boyfriend's father got transferred to Downers Grove, IL, at the end of ninth grade and Kim and Danny broke up, thus ending our immediate circle of friends, not to mention we moved on to high school. From there, I saw Kim a lot because she started dating a guy named Alan. He was a year older than us, I believe, but he attended our small Baptist church and sang in the choir there. Kim would come to meet him at church socials there and after choir practice, etc. She seemed very ahead of her time and sophisticated to me, dating an 'older guy'—again from a teenager's perspective.

> Kim always had a great sense of humor and when she was laughing at something, she usually let off a string of words recounting what she heard that was funny and commenting while she giggled in a higher pitched voice. To listen to it, and watch her, you could not help but join in laughing. In short, her laughter was infectious. But I also remember her as being intense and having strong opinions to contribute to conversations.

Philip Nicholas met Kim at the University of Rochester.

He explains:

> Our other friends Steve and Michael were all on the same floor our freshman year. And then sophomore year, Michael and I moved into a fraternity. It was kind of an artsy fraternity, which is where Michael and Steve and Kim and I really became best friends. It wasn't a romantic or sexual thing in any way. We would hang together all the time. It was actually a really beautiful time of sharing.
>
> Later, I ended up directing a show at the university and I put Kim in it—she was a natural actress. The play was *Chamber Music*, a one-act play by Arthur Kopit. And it's about these eight women in an asylum who have their monthly meeting and each of them thinks that they are a famous character like

Gertrude Stein, Joan of Arc, and Amelia Earhart. Kim played Mrs. Mozart, the wife of 'the' Mozart. So, it's all these crazy women—except maybe Amelia Earhart, who is trying to convince them of who she really is. So it's kind of a cool play.

I don't think that Kim had really acted before, but she was a natural. I heard that she later did news casting for the *Financial News Network*. She was just the kind of person who could probably walk in and get a job like that. She was just a natural—smart and attractive.

I remember that she would be sitting there putting moisturizer on her face and we'd just be talking … she'd call me 'Philly' and she'd start talking about women's sexuality or Anaïs Nin or something deep. That was the kind of friendship we had. She was so full of paradoxes. I mean, she took really good care of herself and loved being a girl, but could also hang with the boys so easily.

She was very intense and passionate, and we'd get into these deep conversations after a couple of hits of pot. (This was 1976 so the pot was really weak, but whatever.) We would talk for hours and hours and play Boston records and a lot of different music. Kim had an interesting taste in music. She was very advanced for her time—probably because of her older sisters. And she would always talk about Lou and Helen and growing up in Westfield, NJ—the suburbs like I grew up in. So we had that in common.

She was intensely interested in relationships and talking about sexuality in relationships. I don't think I ever remember seeing her fall as hard for anyone as she did for Friedland. I think it was the fact he was older and going to be a doctor. There was something about that—because as rebellious as she was, she also liked comfort—so there was this rebel side to her and then there was the Chanel side.

We really had a sweet friendship between the four of us. It was really an innocent time.

A Remembrance

by Lynn Thomas

At the end of the video mentioned earlier, when Kim wishes my parents a happy new decade because they now have a grandson—when I watch it, my heart always aches and skips a beat. That moment, that moment is horrid to listen to and get the depth of her wishes, and to know that the very opposite would occur – not joy, but brutal, heart-wrenching pain, not happiness but darkening sadness, not love but rage at her murderer, not laughter but endless tears, not fun but increasing heaviness at the magnitude of her murder on Elliot, my parents, my sister, and me, our extended family. It was colossal.

Kim and I had discussed many times that we wanted our kids to be close. We said that our kids would spend most holidays together, spend vacations together. Her kids would come north in the summer and mine would go south in the winter. Kim and I had our futures intertwined. We were going to have a business together. We would share with each other the great features a new hotel had that we really liked and would agree that in our hotel or bed & breakfast, we would have the best touches that would make a person or family's stay just extra delightful! We did not discuss exactly what we would do or when, because we had our lifetimes in front of us.

Many people have mentioned at different times in my daughter Carolyn's life, her mannerisms and looks reminded them of Kim. Twice, when I saw her unexpectedly from the side and once when she laughed and threw her head back, I gasped at how much she looked exactly like Kim. I was stunned! When Carolyn was two or three, my mom smiled and commented that she reminded her of Kim. She said, 'She looks like her and is loud like her.' I smiled and nodded in agreement.

My daughter does not know, and will never know her Aunt Kim. They would have had a blast together. Kim would have shared her love of style, makeup, clothes, fun, and they would have spent hours together discussing the latest clothing and style trends. I would just listen in, not being as savvy as they were, and smiling because of the lifetime connections and bonds they were forming.

Kim and I spent many hours playing indoor and outdoor games together. She would almost always win at all card and board games. The luck she had was startling. We would play a tickling game and my idea is that the person who could withstand the tickling the longest would win. When I would tickle her, she would just burst out laughing. She did not care about winning, she just laughed and would start rolling around. She 'lost' according to my rules, but she always won because we laughed.

We would play jacks, jump rope, spud, hop-scotch, and since she was naturally athletic and more coordinated, I rarely won. It did not matter because I always had fun. She never rubbed my nose in the fact I lost almost everything we played or made fun of me because I lacked the natural talents she had. It was irrelevant, we just enjoyed each other.

She told me that when my parents would go out, she and her friends would climb out of her bedroom window onto the roof. Sometimes they would just hang out there and sometimes smoke pot. It was not very slanted, but to me looked like a death-trap. I finally worked myself up to climbing out there, but had my back glued to the house the whole time. Eventually, I felt safer and even a few times enjoyed the escape to the roof.

It was easy to hear when my parents would come home, because the driveway was on the other side of the house. That gave us plenty of time to crawl back in, close the window, and pretend to be engrossed in other things before my parents would even be at the front door.

I remember the Friday morning when Hurricane Hugo hit Charlotte, right after Elliot was born in September 1989. There was a whirring noise and then a loud bang that shook the house. A tree had hit the chimney. Kim, Edward, and Elliot came out of the master bedroom and I came up from the guest bedroom, and we met at the front door. Kim started to cry as she looked out at the damage the falling trees had done to their cars, property, house, etc. Edward said, 'Kim, you wanted new landscaping and look, we got it for free!' She smiled slightly. Friedland continued, 'Don't worry honey, I can earn the money to repair everything in a week, and we will be OK.' She chuckled a bit.

Friedland left the house to find generators for his dialysis machines. He could not drive his car as it was damaged, and even if he could have, no one could have seen the driveway as it was completely blanketed with trees, branches, and leaves. Instead, he walked through the woods to Wendover and I think hitched a ride. Kim and I stayed in the house all day.

We soon learned that some parts of Charlotte had power, so Kim started to make calls from her portable phone to get a hotel for us. The house had no power and thus no heat. Eventually, it got cold in the house. Elliot was too young for his body to regulate his temperature, and thus he needed to be kept warm.

I walked around the house all day with Elliot. I sang to him, cooed to him, rocked him, fed him, burped him, changed him, and loved him all day as his mom and dad were busy. That is the day that I fell in love with him. He was so adorable and sweet, cuddly, easy, and calm. We did go to a hotel and Elliot had the heat he needed to stay warm.

I remember when Kim and I were staying with my parents at the Balsams Hotel in Dixville Notch, NH, in the White Mountains. Kim noticed one of the gorgeous vacation homes on the lake. She wondered out loud, 'I wonder what it looks like inside, and then looking out onto the lake, what is the view from the side window, etc.' Her curiosity grew and when it was clear that the family was not at the house the weekend we were staying at the hotel, she wanted to see if there was an open door. I was a bit horrified. 'What if we get caught?' Kim said, 'By who?' I replied, 'I don't know, the police, the neighbors, the family, etc.?' A bit exasperated with my hesitation and fear, she said, 'Oh, come on Lynn, nothing will happen. Just follow me.' I did because it was Kim. There was a door unlocked. I tip-toed around as she pranced around with joy, admiring many of the beautiful views, furniture, pictures, decor, etc. I know, if we were ever caught, she probably would have talked the police out of any trouble or arrest. She brought much joy to my life when she went for the gusto in many of our adventures.

Kim was my endless cheerleader! She believed in me 100% always and always. When I was discouraged or not sure about something, she would offer a different perspective and it almost always was more positive. I called her Kimmy and she called me Lynny. I forgot that she called me that until recently when one of her friends told me how much she talked about me. Her friend would say enough about Lynny, what about me? Wow! I could feel the impact of her calling me Lynny, right into my heart. The feeling came back. Wow! I remember how wonderful she made me feel. She loved and adored me and I loved and adored her.

After Kim's murder, we regularly visited with Elliot. When he was able, we spoke to him on the phone weekly. We were so blessed to have him visit us three times a year. It was heart-warming to spend time with him in New Jersey or Boston. He was a delightful, easy, and fun boy.

We brought him sledding for the first time, to the racetrack, on boat rides around Boston, to children museums, and zoos, and amusement parks. He loved the train rides in New Jersey and Cape Cod, and we went on a sleigh ride. Elliot was amazed that the restaurant at the top of the Hyatt Hotel turned very slowly. (He tried so hard to stop it!). In NYC, we went to the top of the Empire State Building, visited Madison Square Garden, St. Patrick's Cathedral, and other tourist attractions. He especially loved NYC at Christmas time with all the inventive and colorful Christmas displays.

Unfortunately, when Elliot was 8, Friedland abruptly ended our visitations and phone calls. His attorney said it was temporary, but unfortunately that wasn't the case. I attempted contact for many years and was finally able to reach him in 2007 when Elliot turned 18.

As a gift for his 24th birthday, I wanted him to return to Charlotte where he had some fond memories. He and his girlfriend came, participated in the vigil for the anniversary of Kim's murder, and we all celebrated his birthday together. Afterwards, he decided to move to Massachusetts and live with my daughter and me in 2014.

Together

A Remembrance Poem by Melissa Kassel

We found each other at the age of 3
You led the way with mischievous glee
We built a world together
As adolescents we were wild & free
You were the one I wanted to be
You paved the path to grow creative, creative
Now you are gone the years pass
You live inside of me
You had a smile so tender and warm
You supported me through all the storms
We were supposed to grow old together, together

"Look, Elliot, look … Mom is here with us."

A Remembrance by Michael Verruto

On the first day following Kim's murder, we all gathered at Eddie's mother Josine's apartment. I am not even sure any longer how or when each of us got there. I only remember bodies awkwardly shuffling around in automaton-like stupors, unsure what to do or say next, anxiously awaiting the arrival of Kim's immediate family. Everyone headed to Charlotte immediately upon hearing the news. Lou and Helen, Kim's mom and dad, as well as her sister Lynn had all arrived on the same flight, and were in a car on their way from the airport to meet us. Her oldest sister, Joyce, was flying in from the West Coast, and would be arriving later that afternoon.

My recollection now is that we waited, in rooms heavy and sullen, a collective weight hanging in the air, and around our necks like a yoke; what was wanting to be said, what had been said so many times over, and what must be avoided lest overwhelm and sorrow's barely closed floodgates would burst open again, engulfing one and then another and eventually consuming the entire room. Instead, we each sought earnestly and somehow dutifully to fill the awkward void with:

"Can I get you something?"

"Are you doing ok?"

"I just can't believe this."

"How …?"

"Who …?"

"Why …?"

All except for Kim's deepest love, her little boy, Elliot. To a ruddy cheeked 10 month old, his little round face still flush with another of childhood's relentless sniffles and colds, Mom was just missing. And like any little one would be, he was none too happy over it—restless, fussing, and crying. Inconsolable most of the time. Now, while each one of us hoped, desperately, that he had no idea of what was truly wrong, what horror had actually occurred, one look told you that he indeed sensed something was wrong, something was off, and Mom … well, Mommy's comfort and solace was just not there.

When pain and sorrow is clear on everyone's faces, children will absorb and reflect that energy, even when they don't know why. They can just feel it, and they react accordingly to the fear, stress, and sadness around them.

Here now was the last person to have been with Kim, mere hours earlier in the same home where his new, loving mother was stolen from him, plucked summarily from his life with no warning.

Once everyone arrived and the weight collapsed all the adults to their knees, again and again, it seemed to me appropriate to give them all room to wrestle with this horror, sorrow, and grief, and to give Elliot some space—so I grabbed the stroller, snapped him in, and we headed out the door for some air.

We walked for some time, just the two of us alone, while I just kept a constant stream of talking to him to help seed something in his memory that it would all somehow be okay, some day, some way. Many have called me a "baby whisperer," so I "talked" as I always do, and have done with little ones about everything and anything that surrounded us. And he was responding as every one of them always does.

Sitting totally quiet, as we walked, totally aware, alert and observing everything I was telling him as we walked. The sights, sounds, and smells of a late summer, southern afternoon. A wildflower here, look there's a bee.

"Can you smell the cut grass, Elliot?"

"Mommy loves you, little boy, more than anything in the world; now you just always, always know and remember that." At some point, we saw a small, delicate little butterfly come around us, flitting to and fro, around and around us as we walked. Then two. And then suddenly what seemed like dozens;

small butterflies surrounded us like a light blanket fluttering round and round us both.

We stopped. Enthralled, his little hand reaching out and up, fingers spread wide … Elliot was laughing.

An overwhelmingly clear and intense sensation washed across me; we were not alone. It seemed time itself stood still. Clear now that I was witness to something powerful and moving, I said aloud, almost involuntarily: "Hello, Kim."

The butterflies continued for several moments, one by one leaving to flutter off and away until there was just one remaining. Alighting on the road just ahead of the stroller she floated, slowly moving her wings, as a butterfly will do. Looking, it felt like, straight at us.

We stood there like that for a moment, talking to her until she took off again, circling us once or twice, and then fluttering away into the summer heat.

"Elliot," I said, "Mommy wants you to know everything will be okay, little buddy. And she loves you more than anything in this world." When he turned around and looked at me, eyes wide, a big smile and twinkle in his eye, I knew he had felt it, too.

"Goodbye dear friend," I thought in my heart. "… Goodbye." And we kept on walking, heading back toward the rest of our lives.

"Um, Hello … Is the Doctor in?"

A Remembrance from Michael Verruto

As I sat on the edge of the bed in our master bedroom, attempting to speak to my wife and respond to whatever rapid-fire interrogatory she was peppering me with, I found myself simultaneously in the midst of (yet) another survival round of "ridiculously loud" carousing with my young 4-year-old daughter who, while giggling hysterically, was unceasingly bouncing on same said mattress and box-spring assemblage, then quite effectively launching herself through the air like a medieval projectile to accost my head, neck, and shoulders mercilessly.

Just another evening of our standing, wind-down, bedtime routine (which my poor wife lamented I usually turned into wind-UP BEDLAM … allegedly) that would normally end with my giggling daughter, now wound up like a clock, having refused several times to "let go," would hang across my back like a rucksack, hands slung firmly around my neck, as I transported her into her own bedroom.

Usually.

On this evening, however, as I stood up with her hanging

round my neck as always, there was a loud, stomach-flipping, cringe-producing "POP" followed by the loudest shrieking, crying howling of a wee banshee who had just popped SOMETHING out of socket.

Oh boy.

I am not sure of the exact progress of events that happened immediately after, as it was all a blur. We knew SOMETHING had happened—just not what. Nancy immediately thought of running over to Kim and Eddie's apartment—he was a REAL doctor after all, and could at least see what had happened and if we needed to rush her to the ER or what.

We raced out the door, our daughter still howling in my arms, down the sidewalk two doors away to their apartment, and Nancy rang the bell. What transpired from that moment onward can only be logged in the book of life as one of a father's most ignominious moments. As I held my poor daughter and we awaited the answer to the door I realized, slumping against the brick jamb that I was indeed passing out, tunnel vision closing in, saying "um honey … I think … I'm going down …"

As I came to, my face now ignobly plastered, flat on the cold metal threshold of their now-opened door, what to my wondering eyes did appear, but a diminutive pair of little fluffy pink, what can only be described (as she herself would mirthfully for many years to come, in uproariously retelling the mortifying scene) as "Frou-Frou" slippers.

"Why yes the doctor IS in" came Kim's kind words as the three still-standing adults took our daughter inside to mend, while Humpty Dumpty Daddy peeled himself up again from off their front stoop. Indeed our friends Kim and Doctor Eddie were a blessing for us that night, and made everything right again.

Letter to Kim's Parents from her Neighbor

Betty McCorkle

July 1, 1999

Dear Mr. and Mrs. Thomas,

I live on Churchill Road and knew and loved your daughter, Kim. Many times I have wanted to write to you.

We met in the Churchill Road driveway when you were visiting Kim after the hurricane, Hugo (late in year '89 or very early '90). You may not remember and I may not have the correct address.

But I have a reason to get in touch with you. Even before the tragedy, I kept newspaper clippings on Kim. (She was active and so popular.) I added to these as time dictated.

I'm now 73 years old, widowed, and nearly deaf. I'm planning to move into a small apartment in Sharon Towers, the local Presbyterian Retirement Home. I am having to dispose of many keepsakes. I must do something with my "Kim" scrapbook.

You may not want this kind of reminder. If not, Kim's sisters may be interested. I hope you do want it and that I've not caused you pain.

I loved her very much and treasure my memory of her. I cannot just leave her scrapbook to an uncaring person.

I think of you often. I do hope you are finding some peace. I lost my husband in December 1997 and I miss him very much.

Always, I try to remember God has plans for us and we will all go to be with him in time.

Sending my very best wishes to you along with my "Kim" scrapbook.

I am very truly yours,
Betty McCorkle

Letter to Elliot from Kim's Childhood Friend

Creighton Taylor

July 15, 1991

Dear Elliot,

Writing this letter to you feels like I am standing at the ocean's edge, throwing a message in a bottle into the sea. I don't know when it will reach you, or if (when it does wash up on the shore some years from now) it will provide you with answers to questions you may have about your mother. Despite my uncertainty I sit down to write this willingly because your mother was a special person, well worth your knowing more about, and someone I loved very much. She was my first, and for a long time, best friend.

We went to grade school together and my first recollection of her was from about 4th grade. I was new at school but couldn't help noticing Kim in line during an outdoor assembly – she was up ahead and busy flashing from one spot on line to another talking to different people – she exuded cheerful self-confidence even then, which is assuredly one of the reasons I was drawn to her.

We were in the same class in sixth grade and that is where I really came to be friends with Kim. Our teacher was Mr. Aspenwall. He was an ineffective teacher with a mediocre personality. We relentlessly took turns imitating him, making fun of him, and went so far as doing practical jokes. He had really bad breath and at the time there was a TV commercial for Scope mouthwash in which someone would leave a bottle of Scope and a note "from the Green Phantom" anonymously for someone with bad breath, thereby giving them the message without causing anyone embarrassment. We did the very same thing—leaving a bottle of Scope and a note "from the Green Phantom" in Mr. Aspenwall's desk. We knew he took our advice because later we checked and half the bottle was gone.

I spent many weekend nights at her house and we would do things like run around the living room in our stocking feet and then touch metal things to give ourselves static electric shocks, we played endless games of jacks in the front hall (the tile floor of which she had helped to put in with her father — she took great pride in her home and the ways in which her parents decorated it: the mother of pearl piano in the living room, the newly remodeled kitchen, the tapestry rug in her room, the delicious food her mother cooked, the family vacations to tropical islands, and the family gatherings: all of these were important to her).

We would give ourselves facials, put on make-up, put on records and dance in her room. We went to Love Story together when it first came out and held hands and cried when Ali McGraw was on her death bed. We took walks around the block and talked about life, our thoughts, feelings, ideas, boys, anything and everything. We listened to Simon and Garfunkel on the record player while we were going to sleep, and to Genesis, The Who, Jethro Tull, Led Zeppelin, The Beatles, Crosby, Stills, Nash and Young, The Monkeys, Traffic, Yes, Fleetwood Mac, and The Grateful Dead, among many others.

We used to go "exploring" near her house on Woodends Road—we'd climb around in the deserted area which served as a kind of flood plain between Route 22 and the surrounding suburbs. There was a stream, lots of fallen trees, and a trail, all of which held a great fascination to us as kids. It was like going on a treasure hunt. We rode our bikes up to the Watchung reservation, and especially enjoyed coming back down, going as fast as we dared on the steep hills. Phillip Rudder, who lived across the street from Kim, was a constant companion and playmate of ours, and a special friend of Kim's—essentially a brother.

We knew about each other's first boyfriends. In either sixth or seventh grade, she "went steady" with Chris Bousquet—the cutest, most popular boy in school. They used to go to his house after school and climb up in their big garage, which was more like a barn because it was an old, turn of the century house. They would neck up there and then she would call from home and tell me all about the afternoon they spent together. When I first "went steady" with Jamie Mittendorf (also in our 6th grade class) and got scared after our first weekend of going together I gave the beads he had given me back to Kim, and she broke up with him for me.

Kim was a well-rounded and confident young person. She could do most things well with seemingly little effort. She had a healthy competitive spirit, always trying to do her best. She was immensely popular, both with girls and boys. She couldn't help but realize that she was pretty, had a sensational figure, was bright, intelligent, and vivacious. But even with all these attributes I don't recall her being disliked. She was not haughty or conceited. Some women who are unusually pretty tend to alienate women and only have men in their lives; Kim was not like that and in all the years I knew her I can't remember anyone who didn't like her. She was so charming, engaging, and captivating that people were naturally attracted to her. I think that was one of her finest qualities: She was not only beautiful on the outside, but she was also a warm, caring, sensitive person on the inside and those qualities naturally emanated from her. Kim truly did exude "joie de vivre," and people were attracted to her because of it.

She was very popular with boys and yet I can think of any number of guys who were happy to be just her friend, although I suspect she secretly broke a few of their hearts. That was a special quality of hers—she had good male friends as well as good girl friends.

Kim could also be manipulative and contrary—enjoying her popularity and the "power" she wielded. When we were in sixth grade together she would turn to me and say impulsively "I'm not your friend anymore" and ignore me for the rest of the day. The next day she would act like nothing had happened. She also enjoyed being the center of attention. Her cousin Missy was close to Kim, and Kim enjoyed nurturing a rivalry between us. One time the three of us went to Echo Lake Park and I still remember Kim sunning herself in a rowboat while she reveled in Missy and me jockeying for her approval. In that way I think Kim could be manipulative and self-serving.

Kim was thrown from a motor scooter during one of her family vacations in the Caribbean. She suffered from a pinched nerve in her back and had to wear a brace. She went to a chiropractor for it and suffered from some level of discomfort for most of the time I knew her.

Even so, she was stoic and never complained or cried or even wanted other people to notice—but because I knew her so well I could tell when the pain was bad. She was fiercely proud and independent.

She was a fast runner, athletically strong and coordinated. I recall that in the cafeteria at lunchtime she could out arm wrestle most people, including the guys at the table. She played the clarinet in band, sang in the choir, played the piano, and she enjoyed learning and speaking French—she was always an easy student, doing well with her natural abilities.

Her first real boyfriend was Alan Rasmussen. When they broke up it was because Kim had outgrown the relationship. Alan was heartbroken. It was hard for Kim too. I remember sitting with her on the steps outside the high school right after they had broken up. Alan happened to walk by and Kim grabbed his hand and held it while tears streamed down her face. She didn't want to hurt him, took no pleasure in it, and felt the break just as deeply as he did. But first loves always end and I think theirs was a warm and quite special first relationship.

What I remember liking most about being friends with Kim was how much fun we had together. Kim liked to have fun and was always up for an adventure or new experience. She was so full of life, ready to embrace any new experience with enthusiasm and excitement. We were full of trouble too. We snuck up in the attic at her house and smoked Salem cigarettes;

when her parents went away for the weekend we would have parties and drink beer at her house, we smoked pot: in a word, we were teenagers together.

Her natural good spirits were contagious and we always thought of ways to have fun. I also liked Kim because of her intellectual curiosity, high standards, and artistic spirit. I have one vivid memory of sitting in Kim's room during a rainstorm. I spent so much time at Kim's house that being in her room was not so very different from being in my own, and this storm I sat with my chin resting on my folded arms looking out at the gray clouds, cool wind and gentle rain—the reflective mood of the day infused me with the same spirit of awe and wonder: that is the time in my life when I knew Kim best, when we were just moving from childhood into womanhood and the world was a place full of mystery and wonder. This is what I shared best with Kim, and what I remember most fondly about our time as friends.

I come from a family of five children so there was always a lot of commotion at our house. It was nice to have another home to which to "escape." Kim's family was wonderful to me, including me in dinners out at restaurants (something my family never did), and in general accepting me into the day to day aspects of their lives. In short, I spent a lot of time at Kim's house. When I was in sixth grade my father got cancer (he recovered) and while he was in the hospital I went to Kim's house for lunch every day for weeks. I still remember Mrs. Thomas making us sandwiches and soup and watching a soap opera while we ate. After we were finished we played outside with the other kids on the block. It was a big deal for me not only because I got to ride on the bus (usually I walked home for lunch), but also because someone had a copy of The Godfather by Mario Puzo wrapped in a plain brown cover and we would read the dirty parts on the way home in the back of the bus.

She was a sensitive person too, very loyal to her family. I remember one time when her mother got a slipped disc and was in terrible pain while they got her from her home to the hospital, and Kim was beside herself because she wanted to help somehow. She idolized her older sister Joyce, who was just enough older than Kim to have that effect on her; Lynn was more of a peer—different enough that they could be at odds sometimes, but close enough that they could be silly together. Kim told me once about a Van Cliburn concert where she and Lynn got a giggling fit and couldn't stop, much to the consternation of those around them. She was close to both of them though and had a good relationship with them.

There were a few times when I was there that family differences arose. One time Kim was feeling grief over the recent death of a young cousin from a brain tumor. She was crying and feeling very sad; I went over and put my arm around her and her mother said "No, you leave her alone. She has to learn how to control her feelings." It was hard for me to watch Kim in pain and not do what came naturally (i.e., comfort her) and I could see how she felt conflicted, on the one hand wanting to model herself after her mother's values and on the other hand feeling things deeply and wanting to express herself.

There was another time I especially remember when her father and Kim had an argument. It was over a photo of Kim and her boyfriend Alan Rasmussen that appears in our yearbook. In it they are embracing. When Kim's father saw this picture he just about hit the roof he thought it was so distasteful; he even went so far as to call Kim a slut, and this was very difficult for Kim. I remember walking around the block where she lived and sitting on a rock for a long time while she cried and felt so torn apart — devastated that her father thought this of her, but also feeling full of emotion for Alan and not thinking she had done anything so terribly wrong. She was beginning to emerge as a young woman, starting to define her own values and struggling to rise above the guilt she felt from her father, but confused about how she felt at the same time.

All of these memories of Kim are spokes on a wheel and they all converge, begin and end, in the centermost event of our friendship. I don't really know how to categorize it except to say it was a heartbreaking betrayal to me. When we were juniors in high school I met my first boyfriend. We started going out and after some period of time we became more serious. I introduced him to my circle of friends and obviously to Kim. I don't remember all the details now but at some point I suspected that they were seeing each other behind my back and when I asked my boyfriend, Mark Sullivan, he told me that they had been seeing each other for some time. At first I could not believe Kim would do such a thing but when I realized it was true I told her that I couldn't trust her and that I didn't think I could be friends anymore.

I was in the same homeroom with Kim and spent my senior year trying not to look as humiliated and hurt as I felt. I didn't see Kim much after that, except for one exchange I will never forget. I was in the high school bathroom, having been excused from an Algebra II class because I had broken down in tears, trying to compose myself so I could go back to class when Kim walked in; we were alone in the bathroom and she just walked up to me, started crying and put her arms around me saying, "I'm sorry, I'm so sorry." We hugged and cried and both said that we loved each other. I don't really remember seeing much of her after that and once we graduated we lost touch altogether.

Now that I am an adult and have some perspective on what a terribly confusing, tumultuous time being a teenager is. I am more accepting of what happened. And in all the years that have passed since then I have always thought of Kim fondly and wondered what her life has been like. I always thought that some day I would see Kim again and that we would be able to dismiss that painful episode as part of the "folly of youth" and learn about each other's lives in the present. I don't know if we would have ever been friends like we were as kids, but we would certainly have shared the bond of having known one another during such a powerful, formative time of life.

Kim was my childhood best friend. It is a friendship, I am sorry to say, that did not continue into adulthood. I have felt closer to Kim, and reminded more strongly of her influence on my life, ever since I heard of her death. I had neither seen nor spoken to Kim in well over fifteen years, yet when I got a phone call from my mother telling me she was gone I dropped the phone, stopped breathing, and felt overcome by shock. Kim gone? Kim dead? Even as I sit here to write this I find myself with tears in my eyes, still disbelieving.

I did not know your mother as an adult but everything I have learned about her in the past year from talking to Lynn (who has been incredibly strong and resolute about your having some shared knowledge of your mother as a real person, and not some hollow shrine) seems to echo what was there as a child. She was compassionate, playful, energetic, happy at heart, passionate, loyal, and self-confident enough to pursue whatever she wanted with the intention of getting it.

I have wondered to myself what would Kim think if she read this? Would she think it was true—is this the way she would have remembered too, or is it just my own very personal interpretation of what our friendship was like? Obviously I can't answer that question. I hesitated from writing at all because there are so many other people who knew Kim as an adult, who can answer more fully your questions about her as a person. But with Lynn's encouragement I have tried my best to share with you what I remember about Kim. I only hope this mosaic of memories helps in some way to give you a sense of what your mother was like as a young person.

With warm regards,
Creighton Taylor

Why Kim's Story Matters

"Men are afraid that women will laugh at them. Women are afraid that men will kill them."
~*Adapted from Margaret Atwood and Gavin de Becker*

Some will say that true crime as a genre is hopelessly compromised. They will say it's exploitive, ugly, prurient, voyeuristic. As Susan Sontag wrote in "Regarding the Pain of Others," "No 'we' should be taken for granted when the subject is looking at other people's pain." Her subject is war and its photography, but I think there's a similar warning that true-crime audiences should heed. Any assumption of identification and solidarity is fraught, especially in a world in which white female victims are elevated to an almost cult status, while women of color, who are murdered at a higher rate, are too often ignored.

And yet, in the best true crime there's a quality of the fairy tale or fable: a simple story that reveals powerful, complicated truths. "Hansel and Gretel" is a true-crime story: Their father

> and stepmother abandon them; the witch tries to murder them. Why do children love that scary tale? Because the fear is a thrill, because they can imagine themselves in the same situation and they like the useful advice about bread crumbs and white pebbles. And because in the end justice is served—evil is vanquished and the lost children make their way home.
>
> At the most basic level, true crime satisfies that little-kid desire to see beneath the surface of everything.
>
> ["Why Do Women Love True Crime?" *The New York Times*, July 16, 2019, Kate Tuttle]

There are monsters among us and we know it. However, they're not always who we might think they are. Rarely do we think they are our spouses, ex-spouses, neighbors, or friends. So often we focus on strangers, seedy characters hiding in the dark, and serial killers—those who are beyond belief or sub-human. They capture our collective imaginations, playing on our deepest, darkest fears. But so often, those who are closest to us can pose the most risk—especially for women.

Violence against women remains devastatingly pervasive and starts young, according to new data from the World Health Organization and its partners.

> Across their lifetime, 1 in 3 women, around 736 million, are subjected to physical or sexual violence by an intimate partner or sexual violence from a non-partner – a number that has remained largely unchanged over the past decade.[1]

The United Nations Office on Drugs and Crime reports:

> Women are often killed by someone they know closely. More than a third of femicide victims in 2017 were killed by their current or former intimate partner, and more than half were killed by intimate partners or family members.[2]

The term femicide is said to have been first used in 1801 in reference to "the killing of a woman." Diana E. H. Russell, Ph.D. helped bring the term to popularity during the 1970s. And after making minor changes in her definition of femicide over the years, she finally defined it very simply as "the killing of females by males because they are female." Author Carol Orlock is widely credited with initiating the usage of the term in this context in her unpublished anthology on femicide. There has been a lot of debate over the exact definition of femicide. Jacquelyn Campbell and Carol Runyan use the word femicide to reference "all killings of women regardless of motive or perpetrator status."[3]

For Russell, examples of femicide include the stoning to death of females; murders of females for so-called "honor"; rape murders; murders of women and girls by their husbands, boyfriends, and dates, for having an affair, or being rebellious, or any number of other excuses; wife-killing by immolation because of too little dowry; deaths as a result of genital mutilations; female sex slaves, trafficked females, and prostituted females, murdered by their 'owners,' traffickers, 'johns' and pimps, and females killed by misogynist strangers, acquaintances, and serial killers.[4]

It may seem overly nit-picky to obsess over the precise definition of femicide, but the language, terms, and definitions we use to classify and discuss violence against women is important and likely will be an area that continues to evolve. For Cristina Rivera Garza, a Mexican author, who recently published a memoir about her sister's murder 30 years ago:

> Finding a way to write about her sister's death, even in the context of such pervasive violence, was a challenge. At the time, cases like Liliana's [her sister] were often described in the press and historical records as 'crimes of passion,' a construction Rivera Garza said implicitly blamed the victim while exonerating the accused. This lack of a 'dignified and respectful language' prevented Rivera Garza from writing her sister's story sooner, she said.[5]

Her book *El Invencible Verano de Liliana* was published in Spanish by Literatura Random House last year. An English version, tentatively called *Liliana's Invincible Summer: A Sister's Memoir*, is planned for release in 2023 by Hogarth. "Men kill women because they want to be rid of them, they want to silence them, they want to erase them from the earth," says Rivera Garza.

The numbers and stories are sobering. "Violence is a disabler of dignity, liberty, and rights of the person, with murder being its extreme form for silencing the individual,"[6] write Georgia Zara and Sarah Gino in "Intimate Partner Violence and its Escalation Into Femicide. Frailty thy Name Is 'Violence Against Women.'"

As an active leader in the National Organization for Women (NOW) in Charlotte, North Carolina, Kim Thomas was well aware of the very real and present dangers that threatened women's rights, health, well-being, and lives every day.

NOW has been at the forefront of drafting and advocating for legislation like the Violence Against Women Act (VAWA), which aims to address domestic violence, sexual assault, and harassment, and the many structural issues that allow for the abuse of women with limited consequences.

> Every minute, an average of 24 individuals in the United States are the victims of physical

> abuse, stalking, or sexual assault at the hands of their intimate partners, with 35.6 percent of women in the U.S. experiencing some form of domestic violence in their lifetime.[7]

On July 27, 1991, Kim was honored at a community memorial service sponsored by the Charlotte chapter of the National Organization for Women.

[See article on Kim's involvement in NOW—"That's It For NOW" in *The Charlotte Observer*, September 3, 1989: "What issues rally feminists today? Kim Thomas of the Charlotte National Organization for Women says ERA is on hold; what gets her fired up is abortion rights" on page 258.]

Kim was murdered just as true crime television was coming of age—*Unsolved Mysteries*, *Cold Case Files*, *Dateline NBC*, etc.—which has grown into its own genre of entertainment. In fact, Kim's murder was covered in an episode of *Dateline* in 1998.

Watch the Dateline intro

Murder as entertainment has become a big business—and definitely a disturbing collective obsession. Flipping through channels on television, you will inevitably come across multiple programs about murder, serial killers, and true crime. There's CrimeCon, a true crime convention that attracts thousands, and thousands of true crime podcasters. As of this writing, seven out of the top 10 podcasts are focused on true crime and murder.

In her detailed, two-part article about Kim's murder "Either/Or" in *Charlotte Magazine*, Cynthia Lewis writes:

> Reviewing a few of the American TV crime shows that have recently clogged the air waves, Nancy Franklin has written in *The New Yorker* that 'by solving crimes that often seem mind-bogglingly mysterious or unsolvable,' the programs 'create the comforting illusion that competence—having the right tools for the job—will conquer all; they give us a handle on our chaotic, nonsensical world.' If the murder of Kim Thomas epitomizes that

> chaotic, nonsensical world, explaining it bears small resemblance to a tidy screenplay.[8]

True crime has become so ubiquitous and part of our collective culture that it's easy to forget the people behind these stories are *not* fictional characters. Sometimes it's difficult to remember the real people. As Gillian Flynn wrote in the Epigraph for *I'll Be Gone in the Dark: One Woman's Obsessive Search for the Golden State Killer*: "I love reading true crime, but I've always been aware of the fact that, as a reader, I am actively choosing to be a consumer of someone else's tragedy."

With cases like Kim's and so many others, we become so focused on the circumstances surrounding the victim's death that we forget how they lived—who they were to those who loved them then and love them still. Though sadly that's not what usually grabs headlines. As with all victims of violent crime, Kim's life was so much more than how she died.

These victims are real and their loved ones have suffered an unimaginable loss. Their lives have been irrevocably and horrifically changed forever. They deserve justice and peace.

In a case more than 30 years old, memories have faded, investigators and law enforcement officials have retired or passed away, and evidence has disappeared—but for those who knew and loved the victims, the memories and pain remain.

Inherent in investigating a murder is the unpleasant business of excavating everything surrounding the murder, relationships, vices, and secrets—digging up skeletons, bringing out all the old ghosts, and exposing some very unpleasant aspects of almost everyone involved—the victims, the suspects, and even other family members and friends. In all of us there's darkness and light—for some, one may weigh heavier than the other.

When someone is the victim of a crime, so often we place contingencies around it so we can feel safe: It was a lifestyle choice, a bad decision, they were hanging with the wrong crowd. Regardless, no one ever deserves to be murdered—and not to have someone held responsible just adds to the pain.

It's our hope that through telling Kim's story—who she was during her brief 32 years, those who loved her, the enormous echoing emptiness she left—though now always linked to her gruesome murder, we can help remind people to always remember the real victims and their loved ones. We want to remember how much she loved and was loved.

For all the individuals who have been verbally, sexually, or spiritually abused in any way, we share and honor your pain and anguish. And for those who have been forgotten, fallen through the cracks, or not been given justice as a result of racist, sexist, homophobic, or classist systems, or for whatever reason, we share your outrage.

References:

1: Devastatingly pervasive: 1 in 3 women globally experience violence, World Health Organization, Joint News Release, March 9, 2021 https://www.who.int/news/item/09-03-2021-devastatingly-pervasive-1-in-3-women-globally-experience-violence
2: Rodriguez, Leah. Femicide: Everything You Need to Know, *Global Citizen*, Nov. 3, 2020 https://www.globalcitizen.org/en/content/what-is-femicide-everything-you-need-to-know/
3: Femicide Wikipedia entry
https://en.wikipedia.org/wiki/Femicide, accessed April 1, 2022
4: Diana Russell website
https://www.dianarussell.com/origin_of_femicide.html, accessed April 1, 2022
5: Russell, Benjamin P., "An Author Wrote About Her Sister's Murder. It Led to a Breakthrough." *The New York Times*, March 12, 2022
https://www.nytimes.com/2022/03/12/books/cristina-rivera-garza-book-murder.html
6: Zara, Georgia; Gino, Sarah. "Intimate Partner Violence and its Escalation Into Femicide. Frailty thy Name Is 'Violence Against Women.'" *Front. Psychol.*, September 26, 2018
https://www.frontiersin.org/articles/10.3389/fpsyg.2018.01777/full
7: This Domestic Violence Awareness Month, NOW Demands Reauthorization of VAWA; National Organization for Women; October 2, 2020
https://now.org/media-center/press-release/this-domestic-violence-awareness-month-now-demands-reauthorization-of-vawa/
8: Lewis, Cynthia. "Either/Or." *Charlotte Magazine*, May 31, 2006 https://www.charlottemagazine.com/either-or/

See Louis Thomas' Response to Kim's *Dateline* episode

Afterword

by Cynthia Lewis,
Charles A. Dana Professor of English, Davidson College,
Author of "Monstrous Arrogance" and "Either/Or"

When I first learned of Kim Thomas' death, in July of 1990, my son was three months old. I read the story in *The Charlotte Observer* with horror. Kim, at age 32, had recently adopted a baby boy, Elliot, who was confined to his crib for hours while his mother lay knifed to death on her dining room floor. I knew from experience how much she'd wanted that child after years of dealing with my own infertility issues. Following years of treatment, I had finally become pregnant. I was seized with grief at the thought of what Kim had been forced to give up after her ordeal had at last given her Elliot. How could this happen?

Surely a criminal investigation would quickly yield a perpetrator. But as months, then years went by without a conviction, the prospects of achieving justice grew dimmer. The phases of the case kept coming. In 1994, Kim's husband, Edward Friedland, was charged with murdering her, but the charges were dropped in 1995 when the prosecution's most potent evidence—proof of time of death—was ruled inadmissible by the court. In 1996, Friedland sued Marion Gales for wrongful death. A handyman and known criminal from a nearby neighborhood who had done some yard work for Kim, Gales had been spotted near her house on the morning of her death.

Friedland won the suit, but without solving the case: The bar for proving guilt in a civil case—preponderance of evidence—is lower than that for a criminal case—beyond a reasonable doubt. And Gales' lawyers, weak at best, failed to defend him adequately. Ironically, Gales couldn't possibly afford the huge settlement the jury awarded Friedland. In a final attempt to establish his version of events, Friedland sued the city of Charlotte and four police officers in 1997 for malicious prosecution, a case that was eventually thrown out of both federal and state courts. The murderer still hadn't been convicted.

In 2005, when progress toward identifying Kim's killer seemed indefinitely stalled, I resolved to do what I could to revive interest in the case in hopes that the truth would finally emerge. If I could research the story and publish an article about it in the Charlotte area, possibly someone who knew something would now come forward. As Andy Rosenzweig, former chief investigator of the Manhattan District Attorney's Office, once told me, solving a cold case often depends upon a witness who, having been reticent right after the crime, feels more inclined after the passage of time to divulge information. Potentially, a single such witness could lead to finding and convicting this murderer.

Although I published a two-part article in *Charlotte Magazine* reviewing the evidence against both Edward Friedland and Marion Gales, no one has yet offered an additional clue as to the killer's identity. Yet, I, along with Kim's sister Lynn and Kim's best friend Nancy, continue to believe that the truth will come out. Here's hoping that the Charlotte police will move the case forward quickly, re-interview witnesses, and uncover evidence that will result in long-overdue justice for Kim, her family, and the wider circle of young women and mothers who die by violence. In the meantime, this book, which celebrates Kim and her enormous accomplishments during a life cut short, offers comfort.

In Kim's Words

An Imaginary Conversation with Anaïs Nin, written by Kim Thomas, January 16, 1982

Anaïs: You are a woman—you have 2 paths—either you have children or you don't. I chose not to have any.

Kim: I know. I want to have children. My call in life, whatever it may be, is not an all-consuming one. There is a place for children (motherhood) in my life …

Anaïs: Fine. I have always been an advocate of life … Great experiences, peaks, pinnacles, pits, etc. … People connected are important. Network!

Kim: I am working on beginning a network. It takes a long time to establish friends in a field (first to establish a field) and also to have that openness and follow through—to maintain that network.

Anaïs: Enjoy yourself. Learn from your mistakes. Indulge in your femininity, explore it. It is an everlasting well of fulfillment.

Kim: Yet I feel masculine also.

Anaïs: Explore that—we all have some anima and animas. Know thyself. Learn your strengths and weaknesses. Cater to yourself. Help others and you will be rewarded.

Kim: I must crawl out of my protective shell. Reach out and begin helping others and therefore help myself.

Anaïs: Trust yourself. You will not learn anything if you lie to yourself. So you want children—that becomes a rather consuming task in itself.

Kim: I want that job. I will be a good mother. I will promise in every way possible to give them a fulfilling beginning.

Anaïs: You must find a man. Eddie is a good man but you have not grown very much with him. You must find someone to father your child—who wants to be a father like you want to be a mother. Tell Eddie your feelings and see his reactions.

Kim: What if it is positive?

Anaïs: You have plenty of time before there is any wish involved.

Kim: What else, Anaïs?

Anaïs: Know thyself. Trust thyself, listen to thyself, love thyself. Be good to thyself, and enjoy thyself.

Plus 1: She is wise, isn't she? I get teary-eyed just thinking about how much I've gained through her. I usually sound knowledgeable even though I, myself, am so far behind those last words 'quoted' from her.

Kim's Journal Excerpts

January 1982

[Remembering] It was a time when I was learning about love. When all the mysteries, nuances, hopes and dreams were being realized. It was magical. I was 16, in Nice, France, and falling in love with a Canadian named Peter. I was learning about the art of love, what were the manners, gestures, but more importantly the gentleness, tenderness, honesty, growth, fulfillment of love.

January 1982

Being afraid of the dark, my imagination.

January 1982

It and me are inextricable

It's sort of a nervous, insecure energy that pops up at times.

If it should die then I would be self-destructive for it betters me.

It is the astral betterment of myself.

Together we strive to make me a better person.

A model person - worthy of respect, admirations but humble, always.

February 1982

A little girl asking directions, looking bewildered - about life.

'Is this right? Is that right?'

Still cleaning the murky water,

Standing still so it will settle.

Curious about my sexuality.

Big Eye Inquisitive.

A blossoming flower - beautiful, sweet, fresh and young.

My reflection in the water - young, inquisitive.

But maturing.

Small eye lines.

February 1982

Psychologically / therapeutically helping others.

Exploring my creative capacities piano

artwork

writing

advertising

Learning to say 'no' as my astrologer said.

No to Miami, engagement

No to acquaintances - friends

No to another dinner

No to extra drink

Moderation.

So having moderation, taking control of my life, choosing friends carefully, looking within before thrashing about. More careful & quiet.

December 1982

A cool drink with ice and lime

A gentle breeze

Perhaps some jazz or reggae in the air

Not caught in rush hour

The Lincoln Tunnel

Or clanking typewriters

Four walls with no windows

Free

My spirit wants to be out of the office

But where to go? What to do?

No great talent.

Love Music, like art, Sensitive.

Time - it's on my side.

December 1982

Home

Not a place, but usually so.

I feel at peace and secure

Vanilla candles scent the air

Wind chimes in the breeze

Chime

A hand on my shoulder

Shocked and then smile

Because home, just home

Has touched me.

Nothing like the uprootedness

Jumping at every sound

Insecure, is this alright?

"Do you like me? Or is it my money

That keeps you hanging on?"

July 2, 1985

A Crisis of Sorts.

Don't know if I'm in love with Eddie anymore or if I ever was. Questioning everything!

Work is in an upheaval.

Training as a stockbroker.

Creativity stifled. I'm suppressing aspects of myself and the philosophies and spiritual sides.

Not directed toward any one thing. Very dispersed. Confused. Wondering what happiness means - how to find it/achieve it? Knowing these questions and feelings are OK just torture.
But this is life - these questions are asked by any thinking, feeling individual, Plato, Socrates, Aristotle all wondered about happiness, truths, meaning of life. Feeling like I'm aimlessly thrashing around, chopping - willy, nilly - hoping to get myself back on an even keel.

A decision must be made soon and now I really don't know what I want or need for potential happiness. My life seems to have taken a wrong turn. What happened to Peter, Europe, Fantasy!?

Ohh how harsh reality is for me - how I want to escape these daily doldrums.

Learn some languages and fly away. Live with artists & soak up their creativity, start a small business related to art, music, drama and promote artists.

March 24, 1986

What do I want?

I want a compassionate, sensitive ... aggressive, exciting, stable man who believes in me and adores me, who woos me with flowers and perfume—even after 10 years of marriage. A man who has things in control but who is spontaneous, flexible enough that I don't feel manipulated. A man who has vision and the will to see it through. A doer, a dreamer, a lover.

Eddie says he hates liars, then he hates me and I hate myself because I don't think I love Eddie enough to have his kids, to live our life together. I feel he takes away from me or, well

—I don't know—not right.

March 28, 1986

Came home, called Eddie at Hollywood. He said he thinks our marriage has no future. We are at cross purposes. We see life differently and that maybe we should split up. I think he is right.

Also, I'm not sure if I should go back to Jersey or stay here or move to Atlanta as planned. We will have time apart when I leave for St. Maarten on Monday.

Whispers + Dreams

by Kim Thomas

Hush

Yea let them out

Smile

Oh but careful, those

Dreams die fast

In a wink of an eye or

A drop of blood.

When I was young I remember

in the back seat of an Olds

My sister and I saying who we would

marry and how many children

we'd have.

Lynn wanted a yours, mine and ours family

I wanted just two.

I'd marry for money, Lynn only

for love.

Hush upon the broken dreams

the nightmares that have sprung

Before us we face sterility &

spinsterhood

Two smiling girls lost to

annihilation.

But wait. she now knows that

there is meaning in life, for life

is meaningful alone on its own.

It's all what you decide,

choose & decide

Life

Appendices

911 Call Transcript, July 27, 1990

Charlotte Mecklenburg Police Department *Supplement Report ©*			COMPLAINT NUMBER **19900727215900**	Page # 1 of 4
2. Victim Name **Kim Thomas**			3. Original Offense / Charge **Homicide**	
4. Location Of Offense 3853 Church Hill Rd.			5. Arrest Number	6. C.R. Number
7. Original Report Date **07-27-1990**	8. Supplement Date 10-8-2014		9. Correct Incident Classification	
10. Juvenile Case **No**	11. Multiple Case Clearance **No**	12. Supplement Confidential **Yes**	13. Purpose Of Supplement Interview with Friedland 911 calls	

(unintelligible) 1990. TIME IS 21 HOURS, 58 MINUTES, 6 SECONDS. WILL BE THE FIRST CALL TO 9-1-1.

UNKNOWN: (unintelligible)

FRIEDLAND: Yeah, rush the police to my house. My wife has been killed.

911 OPERATOR: Sir, what's your address.

FRIEDLAND: My wife is dead. 38-53 Church Hill Road. Get to the house fast.

911 OPERATOR: What's your name, sir?

FRIEDLAND: Friedland. Hurry it, hurry it, it's an emergency. I'm a doctor.

911 OPERATOR: Sir, I'm dispatching right now.

FRIEDLAND: My wife is DEAD on the floor. Come here fast!

911 OPERATOR: Yes, sir.

TIME IS 22 HOURS, 5 MINUTES, 2 SECONDS. THIS WILL BE THE SECOND CALL TO 9-1-1.

911 OPERATOR: 911 Emergency, Mcall.

FRIEDLAND: This is Dr. Friedland. My wife is dead. I need help down here. I called you before.

911 OPERATOR: Wait, where are you, sir?

21. UCR Clearance Status] Open] By Arrest] Exceptional] Unfounded	23. Reporting Officer Code Assignment Date **P. B. Rainwater, 2688, Homicide, 10-8-2014**	
22. Investigative Status] Active] Inactive] Closed] Administrative	25. Case Referred To	26. Reviewing Supervisor, Code, Date

Charlotte Mecklenburg Police Department *Supplement Report ©*		COMPLAINT NUMBER **19900727215900**		Page # 2 of 4
2. Victim Name **Kim Thomas**		3. Original Offense / Charge **Homicide**		
4. Location Of Offense 3853 Church Hill Rd.		5. Arrest Number	6. C.R. Number	
7. Original Report Date **07-27-1990**	8. Supplement Date 10-8-2014	9. Correct Incident Classification		
10. Juvenile Case **No** / 11. Multiple Case Clearance **No**	12. Supplement Confidential **Yes**	13. Purpose Of Supplement Interview with Friedland 911 calls		

FRIEDLAND: 38-53 Church Hill Road.

911 OPERATOR: Church Hill Road?

FRIEDLAND: Yes, 38-53 Church Hill Road. I'm waiting for the police.

911 OPERATOR: Okay, sir. Have you talked with Medic?

FRIEDLAND: I spoke with police five minutes ago. Where are they? She is dead! I'm a doctor.

911 OPERATOR: All right, sir...

FRIEDLAND: I need help now!

911 OPERATOR: Sir...sir..calm down, just a minute, okay? You know...just calm down. I'm gonna let you talk to Medic, okay? The police are on the way. Stay on...stay on the line, sir.

<Dial tone, numbers going through, phone rings>

MEDIC: County Emergency (unintelligible)?

FRIEDLAND: Yeah, this is...uh...Dr. Friedland. Listen...

MEDIC: Uh huh?

FRIEDLAND: ...my wife is dead. She's been murdered in my house. Where are the police?

MEDIC: We...we have...uh...Medic and Police en route, sir.

21. UCR Clearance Status] Open] By Arrest] Exceptional] Unfounded	23. Reporting Officer Code Assignment Date **P. B. Rainwater, 2688, Homicide, 10-8-2014**	
22. Investigative Status] Active] Inactive] Closed] Administrative	25. Case Referred To	26. Reviewing Supervisor, Code, Date

Charlotte Mecklenburg Police Department Supplement Report		COMPLAINT NUMBER 19900727215900	Page # 3 of 4
2. Victim Name: Kim Thomas		3. Original Offense / Charge: Homicide	
4. Location Of Offense: 3853 Church Hill Rd.		5. Arrest Number	6. C.R. Number
7. Original Report Date: 07-27-1990	8. Supplement Date: 10-8-2014	9. Correct Incident Classification	
10. Juvenile Case: No / 11. Multiple Case Clearance: No	12. Supplement Confidential: Yes	13. Purpose Of Supplement: Interview with Friedland 911 calls	

FRIEDLAND: They better get here soon…

MEDIC: Oh…

FRIEDLAND: …because it's very difficult right now.

MEDIC: I know.

911 OPERATOR: Dr. Friedland?

FRIEDLAND: Yeah?

911 OPERATOR: Um…I'm sorry, this is 9-1-1 still on the line with you.

FRIEDLAND: Yeah?

911 OPERATOR: Um…I did not take your first call, sir, and I know you're extremely upset. You said she has been murdered?

FRIEDLAND: Yes.

911 OPERATOR: Did you come…

FRIEDLAND: She's handcuffed and it looks like someone blew her brains out.

911 OPERATOR: Uh…sir, did you come in…

FRIEDLAND: I'm a doctor. Believe me…

911 OPERATOR: Yes, sir. Did you come in and discover the body?

FRIEDLAND: Yes.

21. UCR Clearance Status:] Open] By Arrest] Exceptional] Unfounded	23. Reporting Officer, Code, Assignment, Date: P. B. Rainwater, 2688, Homicide, 10-8-2014	
22. Investigative Status:] Active] Inactive] Closed] Administrative	25. Case Referred To	26. Reviewing Supervisor, Code, Date

Charlotte Mecklenburg Police Department Supplement Report ©		COMPLAINT NUMBER 19900727215900	Page # 4 of 4
2. Victim Name **Kim Thomas**		3. Original Offense / Charge **Homicide**	
4. Location Of Offense 3853 Church Hill Rd.		5. Arrest Number	6. C.R. Number
7. Original Report Date **07-27-1990**	8. Supplement Date 10-8-2014	9. Correct Incident Classification	
10. Juvenile Case **No** / 11. Multiple Case Clearance **No**	12. Supplement Confidential **Yes**	13. Purpose Of Supplement Interview with Friedland 911 calls	

911 OPERATOR: Okay. So there is no suspect still on the scene?

FRIEDLAND: I hope not.

911 OPERATOR: Oh, okay, all right, sir. We are on the way to you, sir.

FRIEDLAND: Thank you.

911 OPERATOR: Yes, sir.

MEDIC: Medic's, in route also sir...

911 OPERATOR: All right, thank you.

TIME NOW IS 21 HOURS, 59 MINUTES, 27 SECONDS. BE THE RADIO TRAFFIC ON ADAM 5 TALK GROUP.

WW/olw Corrected on 10-8-2014 by W. E. Ward Jr.

21. UCR Clearance Status] Open] By Arrest] Exceptional] Unfounded	23. Reporting Officer Code Assignment Date **P. B. Rainwater, 2688, Homicide, 10-8-2014**	
22. Investigative Status [Active] Inactive] Closed] Administrative	25. Case Referred To	26. Reviewing Supervisor, Code, Date

The Original Autopsy Report (Excerpted)
Office of the Medical Examiner—Mecklenburg County, North Carolina, Autopsy Report—Narrative Summary

This is a 32-year-old white female who was found dead in her residence on the night 07-27-90 with apparent cutting wounds to the neck.

An investigator from this office traveled to the scene where he noted the body of an adult white female identified to him as that of Kim Thomas Friedland lying face down on the floor of the dining room of the residence, with hands handcuffed behind the back, with body temperature cold and full rigor formation.

Subsequent information from Charlotte Police Department is that the decedent's name is Kim Thomas rather than Kim Thomas Friedland.

EXTERNAL DESCRIPTION

The body is within a body bag and within two sheets and is that of a young adult white female, normally developed and nourished for age, clothed a blood stained light colored silk type fabric pajama shirt. Wrists are enclosed behind the back in a pair of white metal handcuffs. Handcuffs are removed by Charlotte Police Department personnel. There is extensive dried blood over the entire body with the exception of contact points over the anterior legs, very little blood smear on the front of the trunk. There is a small metal bracelet on the right wrist; a yellow metal necklace, chain type, with small pendant containing a clear stone, around the neck. Both ears are pierced and the right ear lobe holds a yellow metal earring with clear stone. There is a white sponge type ear plug in the right ear canal. Fingernails are intact. X-ray of the head and upper chest discloses no evidence of foreign body. External genitalia disclose no evidence of trauma. There are blunt and sharp trauma injuries to be described further below.

PATHOLOGICAL DIAGNOSES

1. Sharp trauma injuries

Multiple deep incised wounds, anterior and posterior neck

Two stab wounds posterior neck

Small superficial cutting wounds: right lip, right upper chest

Shallow cutting wound: right thumb

2. Blunt trauma injuries

Facial and scalp contusions, facial abrasions

Abrasions of the neck

Contusions and abrasions, right and left arms

Small abrasions, back and right hip

Abrasions of wrists

TOXICOLOGY: Blood ethanol (alcohol): Negative

CAUSE OF DEATH: Incised and stab wounds to the neck

The facts stated herein are correct to the best of my knowledge and belief.

(Signed) J. Michael Sullivan, MD, Pathologist, 10-19-90

——

Autopsy showed the body of a young adult female with multiple sharp trauma injuries including multiple deep incised wounds to the anterior neck, multiple deep incised wounds to the posterior neck, two stab wounds to the posterior neck, a superficial cutting wound to the right lip and superficial cutting wound to the right upper chest, and shallow cutting wound to the right thumb. Additionally, there were blunt trauma injuries including scalp and facial contusions and abrasions, abrasions of the neck, contusions and abrasions of the elbows, small abrasions of the right hip and back, and abrasions of the wrists. There was no evidence of significant pre-existing disease. Toxicological analysis of blood taken at autopsy was negative for ethanol.

In my opinion, the cause of death was incised and stab wounds to the neck.

NORTH CAROLINA DEPARTMENT OF ENVIRONMENT, HEALTH, AND NATURAL RESOURCES
DIVISION OF POSTMORTEM MEDICOLEGAL EXAMINATION
OFFICE OF THE CHIEF MEDICAL EXAMINER
Chapel Hill, North Carolina 27599-7580

REPORT OF INVESTIGATION BY MEDICAL EXAMINER

OCME USE ONLY
90-1879
Case number
08-03-90
Date received
☒ Res ☐ NR

DECEDENT: Kim (First) Thomas (Middle) ~~Friedland~~ (Last) (Suffix)

RESIDENCE: 3853 ~~Churchhill~~ Churchill Rd. (Number and Street) Charlotte, NC (City, State) Mecklenbu (County)

AGE: 32 SEX: ☐ Male ☒ Female ☐ Unknown

RACE: ☐ Black ☐ Native American ☐ Oriental ☒ White ☐ Unknown

HISPANIC ORIGIN: ☐ Yes ☒ No ☐ Unknown

INFORMATION ABOUT OCCURRENCE **ALCOHOL: NEGATIVE mg%**

	DATE	TIME	ADDRESS OR FACILITY	COUNTY
ONSET OF INJURY OR ILLNESS	07-27-90	Unknown	3853 Churchhill Rd. ☐ Injury occurred on the job	Mecklenburg
DEATH	07-27-90	10:06pm	"	"
VIEW OF BODY	07-28-90	8:45am	☐ Scene of death ☐ Hospital ☐ Funeral home ☒ Other ME Office ☐ Not viewed	
M.E. NOTIFIED	07-28-90	1:30am	LAW ENFORCEMENT AGENCY: Charlotte Police Department	
LAST KNOWN TO BE ALIVE	Unknown	Unknown	OFFICER TELEPHONE	

AUTOPSY: ☐ None ☒ M.E. Authorized ☐ Non-M.E. Autopsy facility

BLOOD SAMPLE: ☒ Mailed ☐ Obtained by pathologist ☐ Reason not obtained

PROBABLE CAUSE OF DEATH ☐ Pending

1. Incised and stab wounds to the neck
DUE TO
2.
DUE TO
3.
DUE TO
4.

OCME USE ONLY
1.
DUE TO
2.
DUE TO
3.
DUE TO
4.

SDC
☐ None
☐ AI
☐ Dictated
☐ COG

STATUS
☐ NP

MANNER OF DEATH

OFFICE OF THE MEDICAL EXAMINER - MECKLENBURG COUNTY
618 N. COLLEGE STREET
CHARLOTTE, NORTH CAROLINA 28202
(704) 336-2005

SUMMARY AND COMMENT

DECEDENT: Kim Thomas AUTOPSY #: ME-90-1879

This is a 32 year old white female who was found dead in her residence on the night of 07-27-90 with apparent cutting wounds to the neck.

Autopsy showed the body of a young adult white female with multiple sharp trauma injuries including multiple deep incised wounds to the anterior neck, multiple deep incised wounds to the posterior neck, two stab wounds to the posterior neck, a superficial cutting wound to the right lip and superficial cutting wound to the right upper chest, and shallow cutting wound to the right thumb. Additionally, there were blunt trauma injuries including scalp and facial contusions and abrasions, abrasions of the neck, contusions and abrasions of the elbows, small abrasions of the right hip and back, and abrasions of the wrists. There was no evidence of significant pre-existing disease. Toxicologic analysis of blood taken at autopsy was negative for ethanol.

In my opinion, the cause of death was incised and stab wounds to the neck.

REPORT OF AUTOPSY

DECEDENT: Kim Thomas

AUTOPSY #: ME-90-1879
DATE OF AUTOPSY: 07-28-90
TIME OF AUTOPSY: 0845 hours
AUTOPSY AUTHORIZED BY:
J. M. Sullivan, M.D.
M.E., Mecklenburg County

RIGOR: 3+
LIVOR: Anterior, purple
BODY HEAT: Cold
BODY IDENTIFIED BY: Tag
PERSONS PRESENT AT AUTOPSY: Mr. Hughes
AGE: 32 RACE: White SEX: Female LENGTH: 65" WEIGHT: 125 lbs. EYES: Brown
PUPILS: 5 mm. HAIR: Lt. brown BEARD: No MUSTACHE: No CIRCUMCISED: N/A

EXTERNAL DESCRIPTION (scars, tattooing, clothing, property, jewelry, etc.)

The body is within a body bag and within two sheets and is that of a young adult white female, normally developed and nourished for age, clothed in a blood stained light colored silk type fabric pajama shirt. Wrists are enclosed behind the back in a pair of white metal handcuffs. Handcuffs are removed by Charlotte Police Department personnel. There is extensive dried blood over the entire body with the exception of contact points over the anterior legs, very little blood smear on the front of the trunk. There is a yellow metal bracelet on the right wrist; a yellow metal necklace, chain type, with small pendant containing a clear stone, around the neck. Both ears are pierced and the right ear lobe holds a yellow metal earring with clear stone. There is a white sponge type ear plug in the right ear canal. Fingernails are intact. X-ray of the head and upper chest discloses no evidence of foreign body. External genitalia disclose no evidence of trauma. There are blunt and sharp trauma injuries to be described further below.

PATHOLOGICAL DIAGNOSES

1. Sharp trauma injuries
   - Multiple deep incised wounds, anterior and posterior neck
   - Two stab wounds posterior neck
   - Small superficial cutting wounds: right lip, right upper chest
   - Shallow cutting wound: right thumb
2. Blunt trauma injuries
   - Facial and scalp contusions, facial abrasions
   - Abrasions of neck
   - Contusions and abrasions, right and left arms
   - Small abrasions, back and right hip
   - Abrasions of wrists

TOXICOLOGY: Blood ethanol (alcohol): Negative

CAUSE OF DEATH: Incised and stab wounds to the neck

The facts stated herein are correct to the best of my knowledge and belief.

J. Michael Sullivan, M.D., Pathologist
10·19·90

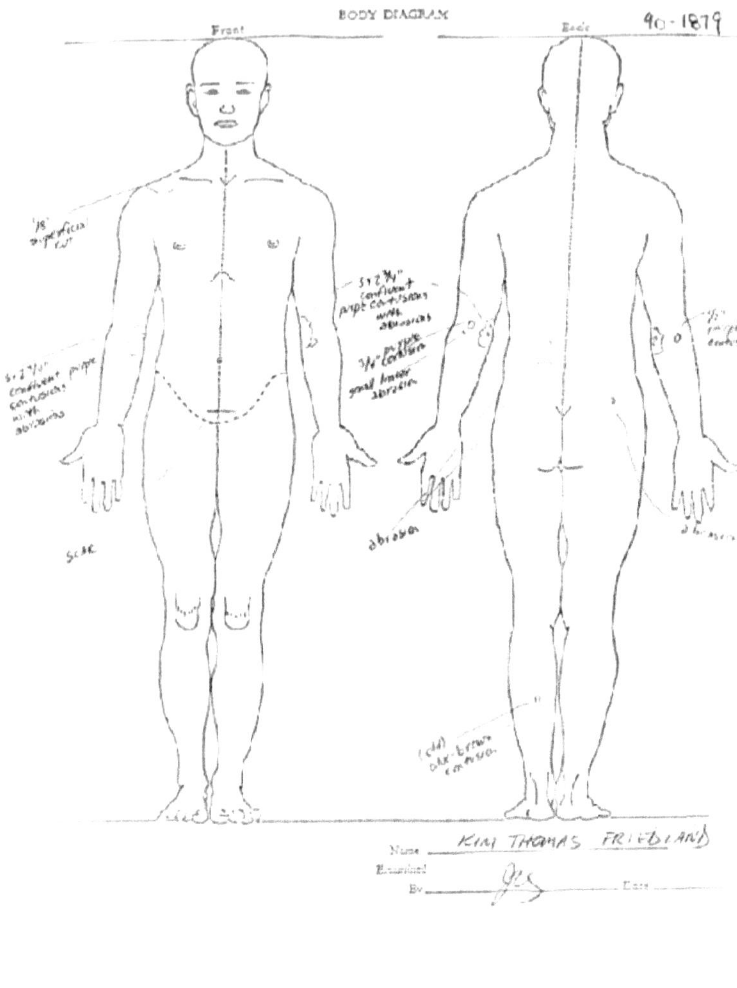
BODY DIAGRAM
Front
Back
90-1879
3/8" contusion
small linear abrasion
abrasion
SCAR
Name KIM THOMAS FRIEDLAND
Examined By
Date

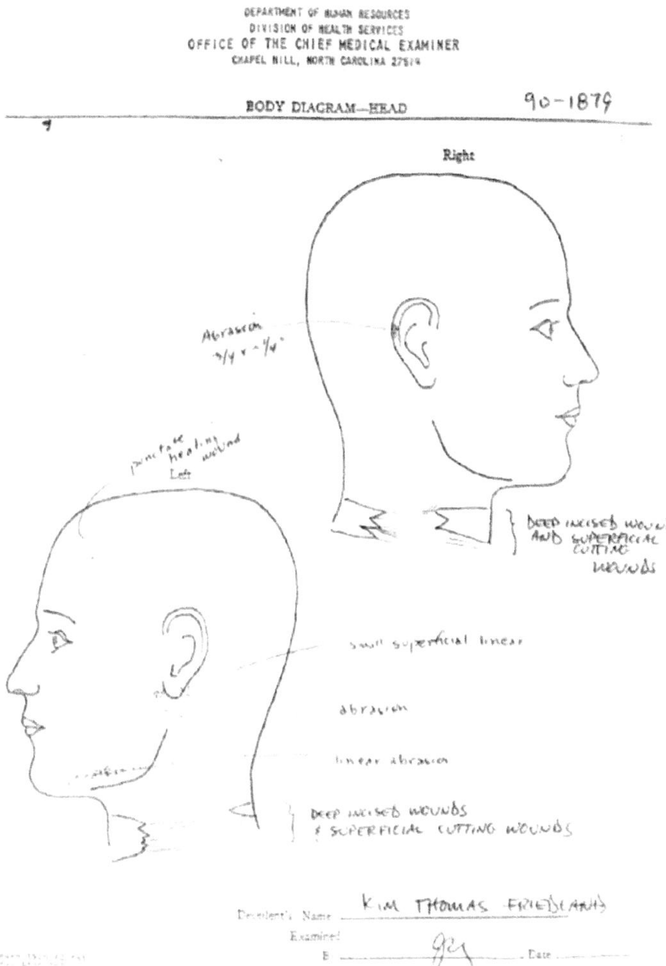

DEPARTMENT OF HUMAN RESOURCES
DIVISION OF HEALTH SERVICES
OFFICE OF THE CHIEF MEDICAL EXAMINER
CHAPEL HILL, NORTH CAROLINA 27514

BODY DIAGRAM—HEAD 90-1879

Right

Abrasion 3/4" x 1/4"

DEEP INCISED WOUND AND SUPERFICIAL CUTTING WOUNDS

puncture healing wound

Left

small superficial linear

abrasion

linear abrasion

DEEP INCISED WOUNDS & SUPERFICIAL CUTTING WOUNDS

Decedent's Name KIM THOMAS FRIEDLANDS

Examined By ______ Date ______

DEPARTMENT OF HUMAN RESOURCES
DIVISION OF HEALTH SERVICES
OFFICE OF THE CHIEF MEDICAL EXAMINER
CHAPEL HILL, NORTH CAROLINA 27514

BODY DIAGRAM - NECK AND SHOULDERS 90-1879

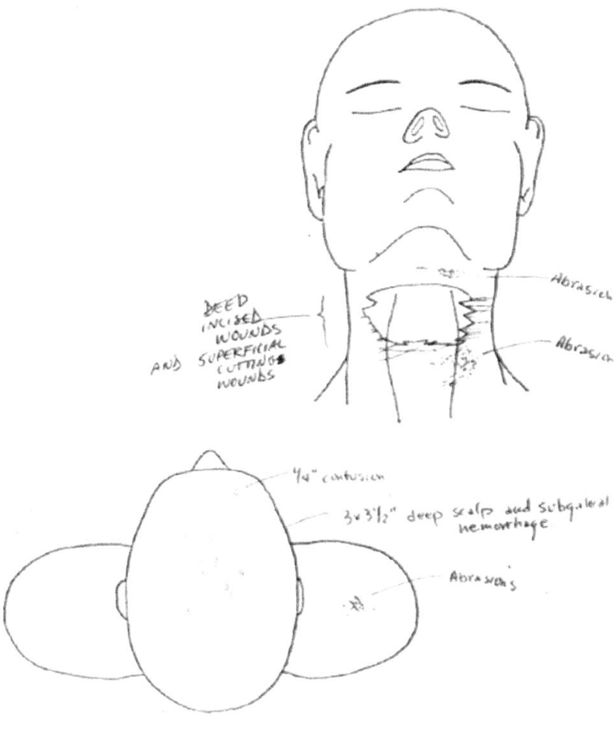

Decedent's Name KIM THOMAS FRIEDLAND

Examined By ______ Date ______

Legal Proceedings Overview

Three Legal Cases in Kim Thomas' Murder Case

First Degree Murder Case: North Carolina v. Edward Friedland – Criminal Lawsuit

Attorney for Prosecution: Assistant District Attorney Richard Gordon

Attorneys for Friedland: Michael Scofield and then David Rudolf

Indictment: District Attorney presents all evidence to the Grand Jury, which decides if there is enough to issue an indictment—warrant for arrest.

July 27, 1990—Kim Thomas is found by her husband Edward Friedland; she is handcuffed and nearly decapitated in the dining room of their Churchill Road home.

Oct. 9, 1990—Friedland announces a private $25,000 reward fund started by Kim's family and friends.

July 12, 1994—Grand jury issues indictment and detectives arrest Friedland, charge him with First Degree murder. He is released on $300,000 bond.

September 8, 1994—Friedland resigns from his medical practice Carolina Nephrology Associates saying he wants to "devote his time to personal needs and his family."

October 12, 1994—Friedland pleads not guilty.

December 1994—Friedland hires David Rudolf as his attorney.

March 20, 1995—At a pretrial hearing, forensic pathologist Dr. Michael Baden says he believes it's "more likely" Thomas died before 7:30 a.m. the time that Friedland says he last saw her alive.

March 22, 1995—The judge rules that Baden can only testify about scientific data; he may not say one time more likely than another.

March 28, 1995—Prosecution drops charges against Friedland without prejudice.

Wrongful Death Action: Edward Friedland, Executor of Estate of Kim Thomas v. Marion Gales – Civil Lawsuit

Attorneys for Friedland: David Rudolf

Attorneys for Gales: Sharon Jumper and three others

March 19, 1996—Friedland files a Wrongful Death Civil Lawsuit against Marion Gales.

November 6, 1997—Jury found defendant Marion Gales civilly responsible for Kim Thomas' murder.

November 9, 1997—Judge Forrest D. Bridges overturns jury verdict for Friedland because the lawsuit was not filed within the two-year statute of limitations.

December 29, 1998—The Court of Appeals of North Carolina reversed the Judge's ruling and found in favor of the Plaintiff Edward Friedland. The jury's decision to award him $8.5 million was reinstated.

Malicious Prosecution Case: Edward Friedland v. Four Detectives and City of Charlotte – Civil Lawsuit

Attorneys for Friedland: David Rudolf

Attorneys for Detectives and City of Charlotte: James P. Cooney III and Charles Tompkins

Summary Judgment Motion: Judgment granted when the pleadings, discovery, and any affidavits show that there is no issue of material fact, there is no need for a trial since there is no legal basis for the Plaintiff's lawsuit = frivolous lawsuit.

June 2, 1997—Friedland files a Malicious Prosecution Case against the City of Charlotte and four detectives in State Superior Court and simultaneously in the US District Court, Charlotte, NC. The lawsuit alleges that the Detectives did not have ample evidence to arrest Friedland and charge him with first-degree murder. He contends that they indicted and arrested him without reasonable grounds.

November 2, 2001—The Judge grants the Summary Judgment Motion for the Defendants which says the Detectives did have reasonable grounds to indict and arrest Friedland.

Defense Overview and Excerpts from Friedland v. City of Charlotte, Attorneys James P. Cooney III and Charles Tompkins

This is a claim for malicious prosecution in which the plaintiff, Edward Friedland, alleges that the defendants, Sgt. Rick Sanders, Inv. Walk Bowling, Inv. Bobby Buening, and Deputy Chief Larry Snider, along with the Charlotte-Mecklenburg Police Department, instituted a prosecution of him for the murder of his wife without probable cause. The plaintiff, however, has conceded that the defendants did not act outside the course and scope of their employment nor did they take actions beyond the scope of their official duties and power.

In this case, the plaintiff must show that a reasonable person would have known that the charge of murder against him had no reasonable foundation—that there was no "probable cause."

"Probable cause" is simply a "reasonable ground for suspicion," which is "determined by factual and practical considerations of everyday life on which reasonable and prudent men, not legal technicians, act."

… It is undisputed that Edward Friedland was indicted for the murder of his wife, Kim Thomas, by a regularly constituted Grand Jury in Mecklenburg Count on July 11, 1994. Following pretrial hearings in March 1995, the opinion of a forensic pathologist that it was more likely that Kim Thomas was killed before 7:30 a.m. on July 27, 1990—a time period during which only Edward Friedland could have committed the murder—was ruled inadmissible.

Subsequently, on March 28, 1995, and based primarily on the fact that the forensic pathologist's opinion had been ruled inadmissible, the State of North Carolina dismissed the charge of murder against Edward Friedland. It did so through a voluntary dismissal, which specifically indicated that the basis for the dismissal was the exclusion of the forensic pathologist's opinion. The 'evidence' against Marion Gales played 'no role' in the decision to dismiss the case against Edward Friedland …
Subsequently, James Cooney noted in his Summary Judgment that Judge Gary probably made an error in dismissing all of Baden's testimony. He should have only excluded the portion about the last statement alluding to vitreous potassium fluid and allow the remainder in as evidence.

The District Attorney of Mecklenburg County—who authorized the dismissal—testified that when the charge was dismissed, there was probable cause to believe that Edward Friedland had killed Kim Thomas and, in fact, there were 'a series of circumstances that were well beyond probable cause.'
The dismissal was taken because the District Attorney was concerned that without the testimony of the forensic pathologist, Edward Friedland might be acquitted of this crime and could

never be retried for the murder of his wife again, regardless of his actual guilt.

> [The Double Jeopardy Clause in the Fifth Amendment to the U.S. Constitution prohibits anyone from being prosecuted twice for substantially the same crime.]

In explaining his decision to dismiss this charge to Kim Thomas' family, the District Attorney wrote:

One of the primary factors which led us to enter the dismissal was that if we had not done so, and if the case had proceeded to trial resulting in a dismissal by the trial judge, Dr. Friedland could never be charged in this murder case, even if further incriminating evidence were to turn up … I do not believe any competent responsible prosecutor would have continued on with this case, knowing that a possible murderer might thereafter be protected from ever being prosecuted again for his crime.

… Nonetheless, Edward Friedland now claims that his prosecution for the murder of his wife was initiated by the defendants without probable cause.

Overview

On the evening of July 27, 1990, Edward Friedland called 911 to report finding Kim Thomas' body in their home. For the next four days, investigators processed Kim Thomas' house, collecting more than 100 pieces of evidence in addition to hundreds of hairs and fibers, making more than 400 photographs of the crime scene and surroundings, videotaping the crime scene, conducting chemical and scientific tests for blood, fingerprints, and biological material, and conducting grid searches of the area surrounding the house in a search for evidence relating to the murder. Over the next four years, 119 witnesses were either interviewed or provided information to investigators, hundreds of forensic tests and analyses were performed on the evidence collected from the crime scene, and experts in blood spatter interpretation, forensic pathology, crime scene and victim profiling were consulted from the State Bureau of Investigation, the New York State Police Lab, and the Federal Bureau of Investigation. Ultimately, more than 50 officers, investigators, crime-science technicians, and laboratory personnel of the Charlotte-Mecklenburg Police Department participated in the investigation into the murder of Kim Thomas.

The undisputed facts that emerged from the investigation of Kim Thomas' murder from July 27, 1990 through March 28, 1995, led to the conclusion that only Edward Friedland had a motive to see Kim Thomas dead, that Edward Friedland had the opportunity to commit this murder, and that the evidence at the crime scene virtually eliminated a stranger or an intruder bent on robbery as the motive in this case:

Motive: Throughout his marriage to Kim Thomas, Edward Friedland regularly deceived and cheated on her. Less than one year before her murder, Edward Friedland consulted with an attorney about divorcing Kim Thomas because his then-mistress was pregnant. Once he learned that the financial cost of a divorce would be 'unacceptable,' Edward Friedland stayed in the marriage and continued his affair. In the month before her murder, Kim had talked with others about leaving Edward Friedland and, five days before the murder, Edward Friedland learned that his affair was becoming public.

Opportunity: Edward Friedland did not leave his home until approximately 8 a.m. on July 27. Based on the condition of her body, the fact that she was found wearing her bedclothes and sleeping earplugs, and that she did not do her regular morning activities, the medical examiner informed investigators that Kim Thomas was likely killed in the early morning of July 27. A forensic pathologist consulted by investigators concluded that Kim Thomas was likely killed before 7:30 a.m. Edward Friedland was the only person who could have murdered Kim Thomas before 8 a.m.

The Crime Scene: There was no forced entry, robbery, sexual assault, or burglary. Based upon the location of both visible and chemically enhanced blood stains, it appeared that the killer was familiar with the house, that the killer may have cleaned himself at the house, that the killer took the time to search through a number of items in the house and to turn on and off lights and close doors behind him, but that the killer stole nothing of value. Several of the investigators and consultants believed that the killer manipulated the crime scene in an attempt to suggest robbery as a motive. In addition, human blood—which was likely Kim Thomas'—was found in Edward Friedland's car.

Edward Friedland: When Edward Friedland was interviewed by investigators shortly after reporting his wife's murder, he was calm, unemotional, he was speaking with a number of different people by telephone, and was able to give a detailed alibi. Edward Friedland did not go to his wife's body or even enter the room in which she was found; however, he described details of her body and of the room where he saw her body that investigators did not believe could have been seen in the dark from his position in the house. As the investigation progressed and questions were raised concerning the state of his marriage and affairs, Edward Friedland became uncooperative and evasive with investigators and contradicted himself on several critical points, including whether Kim Thomas was even awake when he left his home.

In short, the undisputed facts in this case pointed unerringly and plainly to the conclusion that there was probable cause to believe that Edward Friedland murdered Kim Thomas in the early morning hours of July 27, 1990.

Conclusion

In any criminal case, much less a murder case, there is a temptation to evaluate evidence in the context of reasonable doubt—to ask whether the evidence can establish to a moral certainty the guilt of a suspect. While that would certainly have been the standard for the Jury had the prosecution of Edward Friedland gone forward, it is not the standard for this Court on this claim. Rather, as noted at the outset, the issue here is whether these facts establish the fair probability that Edward Friedland killed his wife; whether they create "reasonable grounds" to believe that he committed this crime.

In this respect, and unlike the task presented to a jury sitting in a criminal case, this Court's task is relatively simple. There is ample evidence that Edward Friedland had the motive to kill his wife to prevent "a loss of a lot of what I had worked for"—the same motive that prevented him from leaving his wife. There is no dispute that he had the opportunity to commit this murder—indeed, he is the only person who can definitively be proven to have been in the house during the time that Kim

Thomas was likely killed. Finally, Dr. Michael Baden's opinion that it was more likely that Kim Thomas was killed before 7:30 a.m.—when Edward Friedland was alone with her in the house—plainly creates probable cause to believe that Edward Friedland committed this murder.

In the amended complaint, and throughout the course of this litigation, the plaintiff has directly attacked the integrity, honesty, competence and veracity of both the individual defendants and the Charlotte-Mecklenburg Police Department. He has done this to establish his claim that the defendants acted with the "actual malice" sufficient to entitle him to an award of punitive damages. However, allegations of malice do not prove a lack of probable cause.

The facts revealed by the nearly three years of discovery conducted by the plaintiff in this case show absolutely no bias, prejudice, or animus toward Edward Friedland by the Charlotte Police Department before the murder of his wife. Indeed, Edward Friedland was completely unknown to the police until his first 911 call on July 27, 1990. The plaintiff has found no evidence that police conspired to accuse Edward Friedland of this crime because they bore him ill will or prejudice. Instead, the evidence has shown plainly and unequivocally that the police investigated Edward Friedland because of a good faith belief that he was the murderer.

Had the police wished to act on the basis of prejudice, appearance, and animus, there was a suspect readily available—Marion Gales. That Marion Gales was set aside as a suspect in this case in the weeks following this murder was not a result of the fact that the police "liked" Marion Gales; rather, it is uncontroverted that Marion Gales was not pursued because the police did not believe he committed this crime. In short, Edward Friedland was investigated by the police because that was where the evidence led …

Who's Who

Fita Alfaro	Housekeeper
Dr. Thomas Andrew	Medical Examiner/NH
Dr. Michael Baden	Forensic Pathologist/NY
Charlie Barkley	Business Attorney/Charlotte
Brendan Battle	Private Investigator (hired by Lou Thomas)
Buzz Boothe	Homicide Detective
Walter Bowling	Homicide Detective
Dr. John D. Butts	Medical Examiner (former, Chief of NC State)
Judge Forrest D. Bridges	Marion Gales Wrongful Death Trial
Sara Briggs	Elliot's Babysitter
Jan Ellen Brown	Kim's Friend/Charlotte
Lauren Brown	Kim's Friend/Infertility Piedmont/Charlotte
Robert Buening	Homicide Detective

Jim Clarke	Edward's Friend/ Best Man at first wedding
Jim Cooney	Attorney for City of Charlotte/Malicious Prosecution Case
Bridgette Davis	Edward's Girlfriend/Nurse
Dr. K. Dunbar	Edward's Business partner in Charlotte
Judge B. Craig Ellis	Malicious Prosecution case/ Charlotte
Kathy Fletcher	Bridgette David's Friend/Nurse
Elliot Friedland	Kim's and Edward's son
Josine Friedland	Edward's Mother
Lesley Friedland	Edward's Sister
Lisa B. Friedland	Friedland's Second wife
Nichole L. Friedland	Edward's Third Wife
Marion Gales	Defendant in Wrongful Death Action/Charlotte
Peter Gilchrest	District Attorney (1990-2011)/Charlotte
Melissa Gilman	Edward's Sister

Richard Gordon	Assistant District Attorney/Charlotte
Sally Gordon	Social Worker for Kim and Edward during adoption
Judge Marvin K. Gray	Pre-trial hearings for murder case against Friedland
Dr. W. Greenberg	Anesthesiologist/Charlotte
Ron Guerette	Private Investigator (hired by David Rudolf)
Bryan Guidroz	Hair Stylist/Charlotte
Edward Hinson	Attorney/Charlotte (hired by Louis Thomas)
Bob Holl	Homicide Detective
Jim Hollingsworth	Homicide Detective
Ken Holt	Friedland's Business Partner
Dr. Page Hudson	Medical Examiner (former Chief, State of NC)
Dr. Charles Hughes	Medical Examiner/Charlotte
Chris Jones	Nurse/Charlotte
Sharon Jumper	Attorney for Marion Gales civil case
Melissa Kassel	Kim's Cousin

Laurie Schramm Levites	Kim's childhood friend
Elizabeth Leland	Journalist, *Charlotte Observer*
Cynthia Lewis	Author, Professor, Davidson College
Kelly Ann Liebling	Elliot's Nanny
Thomas K. Maher	David Rudolf's Law Partner
Suzanne Mallis	Neighbor/Miami
Spencer Merriweather	District Attorney (2017-present)/Charlotte
David M. Moore	Neighbor/Charlotte
Andrew Murray	District Attorney (2011-2017)/Charlotte
Philip Nicholas	Kim's Friend/University of Rochester
Kay O'Neill	Elliot's Babysitter
R. Peak	Luminol expert
Judy Pearlman	Kim's Friend/University of Rochester
Sherry Picker	Kim's Friend/Miami
Darrell Price	Head of Cold Case Unit (thru 2020)

Donald Rock	Robbery/Burglary Detective
Philip Rudder	Kim's Childhood Friend/NJ
David Rudolf	Friedland's Criminal Defense Attorney/Charlotte
Steve Schramm	Childhood friend
Sgt. Rick Sanders	Supervisor of Homicide Division/Charlotte
Michael Scofield	Friedland's Criminal Defense Attorney/Charlotte
Ellyn Silverman	Kim's Friend/Charlotte
Michael Sloop	Head of Cold Case Unit (2021-Present)
Larry Snider	Chief of Homicide Division/Charlotte
Nancy Steiffel	Kim's Friend/University of Rochester
Margie Storch	Kim's Friend/NOW/Charlotte
G. Barnett-Streicher	Nurse/Charlotte
Dr. J. Michael Sullivan	Medical Examiner/Charlotte
Creighton Taylor	Kim's Childhood Friend/NJ
Roberta Tepper	Assistant District Attorney
Caroline G.K.H. Thomas	Kim's Niece

Helen F. Thomas	Kim's Mother
Joyce L. Thomas	Kim's Sister
Louis J. Thomas	Kim's Father
Lynn M. Thomas	Kim's Sister
Bruce Treadway	Police Captain/Charlotte
Robin Underwood	Friend/Charlotte
Brenda Veigh	Elliot's First Nanny
Nancy S. Verruto	Friend/Charlotte
Michael Verruto	Friend/Charlotte
Jack Wolfe	Retired District Attorney/Charlotte

Crime Scene Images

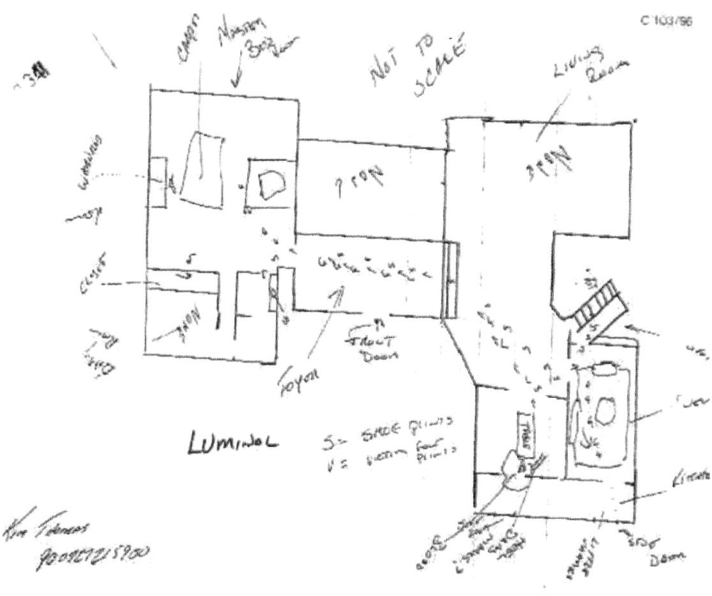

Floor plan of 3853 Churchill Rd., Charlotte, NC

Front entrance, Churchill Rd.

Master bedroom, July 1990

Blood droplets on floor (entering kitchen from dining room)

The body of Kim Thomas on the dining room floor

Smeared blood, dining room floor
(door to kitchen on the far right)

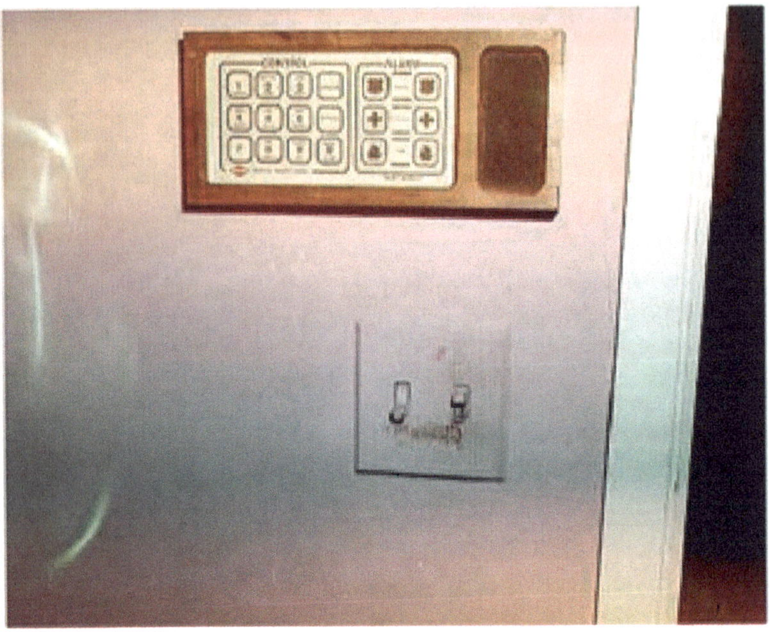

Master bedroom light switch (blood smear the length of a forefinger on switch plate directly under toggle switches)

Blood smears on Edward Friedland's armoire

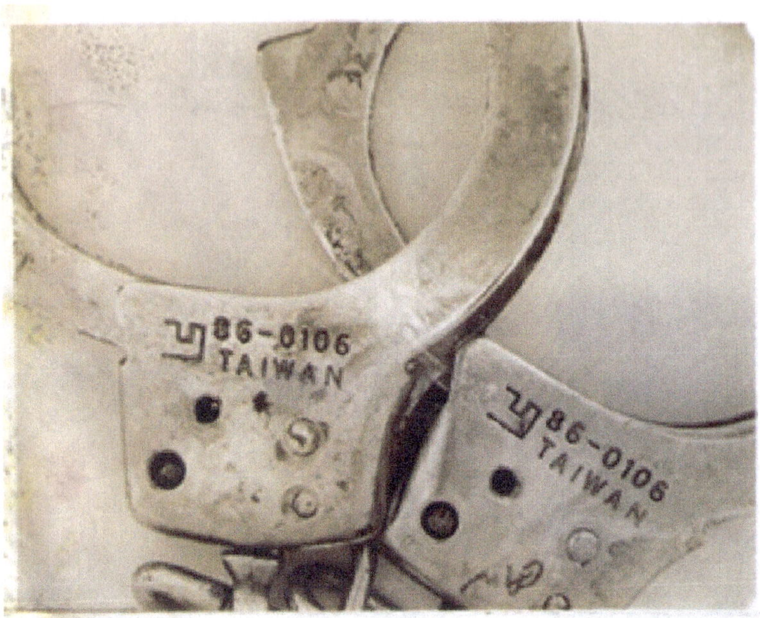

Handcuffs removed from Kim's hands, post-mortem

The crime scene, 3853 Churchill Road, July 1990

Selected Television News Coverage of Kim's Murder and the Investigation

Print News Coverage of Kim's Life and Murder

Kim Thomas, a leader with Charlotte's chapter of the National Organization for Women, says, "We're for basic rights and family and women to be able to make private decisions about how many children they want to have in their families."

What issues rally feminists today? Kim Thomas of the Charlotte National Organization for Women says ERA is on hold; what gets her fired up is abortion rights.

That's It For NOW

By MELISSA WALL

During the past 18 months, Kim Thomas underwent three operations, took fertility drugs and tried in-vitro fertilization. She still couldn't get pregnant. Early this month, she and her husband, Edward Friedland, will adopt an infant boy from his Texas birth mother.

Thomas says though it may seem ironic, she still believes in abortion.

"Even though I don't have the choice — to tell any other person what to do with her body seems so unconscionable to me. I don't understand how one woman could say to another woman, 'You have to bear this life.'"

Thomas, 31, is a member of the Charlotte National Organization for Women leadership circle; her task is to share information from the state and national levels with local members. There are no officers. The 10-member circle "is a more feminist way of distributing power," Thomas explains.

Charlotte NOW formed in 1972 when 100 people attended an organizational meeting. Demands then ranged from job advertisements that did not specify sex, to pay for homemakers. Attempts to ratify the equal rights amendment fueled the organization throughout the '70s.

Thomas says such an amendment would make a difference with the pressing women's issue of today: the right to have an abortion, now threatened with restrictions because of a July Supreme Court decision.

Sitting in her southeast Charlotte

See NOW Page 3E

In July, NOW and Concerned Charlotteans for Women staged a protest at Freedom Park, denouncing President Bush's call for an amendment to protect the flag. Believing Bush should be focusing his attention on women's issues, the groups wrapped a mannequin in chains.

'We're Not Crazed Feminists'

Here is what Kim Thomas, a leader in Charlotte's National Organization for Women chapter, has to say about abortion rights and other issues before the organization:

Q. In July, the Supreme Court ruled in Webster vs. Reproductive Health Services that states are free to restrict abortions. In the months surrounding the controversial decision, the National Organization for Women's national membership rose dramatically from 160,000 last year to more than 200,000. Charlotte NOW's membership has gone from 88 before the decision to 116 today. Why?

A. It's become much more mainstream. We're not the radical, bra-burning, crazed feminists who want men to share 50/50 in their household work and cook three times a week. We're for basic rights and family and women to be able to make private decisions about how many children they want to have in their families.

And that's apple pie. That's not something anyone's afraid of.

I've been getting calls since the Webster decision from mill workers to professional women to housewives, mothers at home. It's really all across the board.

Q. Does Charlotte have enough people who agree with NOW's thinking to support the local organization?

A. I think it's a problem with so many fragmented women's groups. We have the Women's Political Caucus, we have NOW, we have Coalition for Choice and then we have other ad hoc groups. We sort of all have the same platform. That creates a lot of division, and I think one of the things that's kept women down for all those centuries is that we are divided.

We have our children. We have our families. We have our work. We have our church or our temple. We have so many different places that we need to be. That's just a great way of keeping women down and keeping them oppressed.

Q. On July 3, 25 men, women and children took part in a demonstration at Freedom Park organized by Concerned Charlotteans for Women,

See WE'RE Page 3E

THE CHARLOTTE OBSERVER Sunday, September 3, 1989 3E

'We're Not Radical, Crazed Feminists,' NOW Leader Says

Continued From Page 1E

a coalition of women's groups including NOW. A chained mannequin was gagged by an American flag. It held a "bloodstained" coat hanger in one hand and an "ERA Yes" banner in the other. The protest was in response to President Bush's call for an amendment to ban burning the flag and what the protesters saw as his lack of attention to women's issues.

Do actions have to be flashy to rally your members or keep people interested?

A. At our meetings sometimes there are 20 people, sometimes up to 50. But the momentum doesn't stay. We may need to have continuous actions and keep the issues alive. . .

If we have people who start coming to the meetings and start getting enthusiastic and excited about planning these actions and who are out there. . .

If you have just a core group of six burned-out people that really can't do any more, you're not going to get the exposure, and your profile will stay low.

Q. Is it hard for you with your status in the community as the wife of a doctor — as opposed to the radical student you once were — to step up and say, "I have this opinion" or to participate in a march — to make waves?

Early this month, Kim Thomas and her husband, Edward Friedland, will adopt an infant boy from his Texas mother. Thomas says, "As an adoptive parent who's pro choice, I have a very personal understanding of the issue."

NOW Leader Focuses On Legal Abortion

Continued From Page 1E

home. Thomas talks in clipped words about her childhood in Westfield, N.J. One memory still burns. "I was 12, a budding adolescent. I used to play football. We had jerseys, shoulder pads, the whole regalia." That year her father told her she couldn't play anymore because she was a girl.

Woman Found Slain In Her Southeast Charlotte Home

By NANCY WEBB
Staff Writer

Homicide officers early today were investigating the death of a woman whose body was found in her southeast Charlotte home.

"The trauma to the body indicates it probably was not suicide," said Charlotte police Cmdr. Bruce Treadaway.

The woman, Kim Thomas Friedland, 31, had head and upper body injuries, Treadaway said. Her body was found in the dining room just off the main entrance.

Edward Friedland, a general practitioner, told police he came home from work about 10 p.m. Friday and found his wife dead in their Churchill Road home.

Their baby, who police said was about 18 months old, was in another room and crying when police arrived. No one else was home at the time.

About 11:15 p.m., a man escorted by police walked out of the house carrying the baby, wrapped in a white blanket. The baby had not been harmed, police said.

Early today, investigators were setting up lights in the Friedlands' yard to search for evidence before heading inside. The house sits at the end of a driveway that winds through woods in the upper middle-class neighborhood. The back of it faces Wendover Road.

As Son Cried, Activist Found Beaten In Home

By JOHN MINTER
And VALCA VALENTINE
Staff Writers

Kim Thomas knew life as a TV analyst, author and activist for women's rights, but 11 months ago she added something she had longed for.

Thomas, 32, and her husband, a physician, adopted an infant after years of trying to conceive.

But those months of joy as a mother came to an abrupt and shocking end.

Thomas, who helped lead the Charlotte chapter of the National Organization for Women, was found beaten to death Friday night inside her home in southeast Charlotte off Wendover Road.

Thomas' husband, Dr. Edward Friedland, told police he arrived home about 10 p.m. to find his wife dead in the dining room and the couple's 13-month-old son, Elliot, crying in his crib.

Police said Saturday they have few leads and no suspects in the killing, which stunned the couple's friends and neighbors.

File/DON STURKEY

Kim Thomas holds her Yorkshire terrier, Rags, during a Charlotte Observer interview at her home last August.

"I'm just shell-shocked," said Caroline Elliot, a neighbor. "You read about things like this happening, but this just brings it home, the ugliness in the world. Just the enormity of what happened makes my blood run cold."

"All the people I've talked to today are devastated and shocked," said Charlotte Brody, a friend and president of Planned Parenthood of Greater Charlotte. "The terror she must have gone through. There is no way around the gut-level fear that you have to feel about a woman at home taking care of her baby and being beaten to death."

Police said Thomas apparently fought with her attacker. They were unsure when she was killed. An autopsy was under way late Saturday.

"There's some evidence of a real violent struggle," said police Cmdr. Bruce Treadaway. "We don't have any eyewitnesses or motive at this particular time. Those things do pose a very big problem."

Friedland told police he last spoke to his wife before leaving home for work at 7 a.m. Friday. When he returned Friday night, he heard his son crying from outside the house.

He said he went directly to his son's room to comfort him, then looked for his wife and found her dead on the dining room floor.

Friedland was staying at another Charlotte home with family members Saturday and declined to be interviewed.

See FRIENDS Page 13A

Slaying Chills Southeast Neighbors

Who Was Kim Thomas?

- Co-author, with Nancy Styles Verruto, of "A Charlotte Child: A Guide for the Pregnant Woman."
- In Leadership Circle of Charlotte chapter of National Organization for Women.
- Former stockbroker in Miami, appeared regularly on the Financial News Network. Moved to Charlotte in 1986.

MARK B. SLUDER/Staff

A Charlotte police officer keeps watch on North Wendover Road where the home of Kim Thomas, on Churchill Rd., can be seen through the trees. Friday night, Thomas' husband found her beaten to death on the dining room floor of the home.

THE CHARLOTTE OBSERVER Sunday, July 29, 1990 13A

Friends 'Devastated And Shocked' At Slaying

Continued From Page 1A

Officers found no sign of a break-in and nothing was known to be missing from the house, Treadaway said. Thomas' burgundy Mercedes station wagon was parked outside.

Investigators and crime scene technicians used floodlights Friday night and early Saturday to search for clues in and around the gray wood-frame house at 3853 Churchill Rd., off Wendover Road. The house sits on a wooded lot in the secluded neighborhood of 1950s homes.

A team of five investigators, headed by Sgt. Rick Sanders, remained at the scene until Saturday afternoon. At one point, 10 uniformed officers spent more than an hour combing through the surrounding woods.

Police planned to allow Friedland into the home today to confirm that none of the couple's possessions are missing. Treadaway urged anyone who saw or talked with Thomas on Friday to call Crimestoppers, 334-1600, anytime.

The couple's home has been burglarized twice since they moved there in 1986, Treadaway said. Neighbors said break-ins are not uncommon in the neighborhood.

"We have bars on our doors now," said resident Robert McCorkle, 24, who grew up nearby. "Over the years things have changed. A lady that lived next door was shot during a break-in a few years ago."

Elliot said her home was broken into twice, most recently about four years ago. "The people were in the house when we came down the driveway," she said. "They just broke down the back door and ran into the woods."

As police worked to find Thomas' attacker, friends recalled her dedication to women's causes, especially the National Organization for Women. She was the local chapter's information coordinator.

"She was our contact person," said NOW member Marjorie Storch. "She really held things together for us in the past several years. . . . She believed deeply in justice and spent a lot of hours working for justice."

Donna Arrington remembered how her friend would help with consciousness-raising for a women's study group at UNC Charlotte. "She did not mince her words but was straight to the point. But she said it with a smile, in a very loving way. She had a real vitality about her."

Thomas also co-wrote with Nancy Styles Verruto a manual, "A Charlotte Child: A Guide for the Pregnant Woman," published in April 1988.

While she worked on the book, Thomas and Friedland tried without success to have a child. She underwent three operations and tried fertility drugs and in vitro fertilization.

In April 1989, they decided to adopt. They went to Texas, which has liberal adoption laws, and arranged with an expectant mother to adopt her infant.

"They brought the baby home just before Hugo," neighbor Elliot said. "They were without power for three weeks and she went to stay in a motel. We said she should change his name to Hugo."

Before moving to Charlotte in 1986, the couple lived in Miami,

Charlotte homicide investigators stand in the drive of the victim's home. Sgt. Rick Sanders (center) is heading the investigation. An autopsy was under way late Saturday.

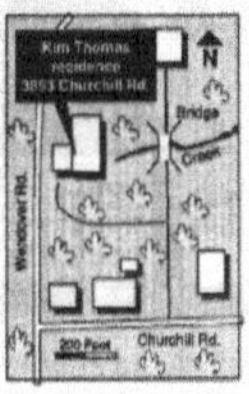

where Thomas was a stockbroker and appeared regularly as an analyst on cable television's Financial News Network.

Neighbors described the petite, dark-haired woman as a friendly sort who waved to others as she walked or drove along the couple's 100-yard driveway to their home in a wooded area.

"Kim was an exceptional lady," said McCorkle.

Elliot, who hadn't seen Thomas since last week, recalled watching Thomas walk her baby and her dog, a Yorkshire terrier, "who just fit her."

"Her baby was named Elliot and they spelled it with one T," Elliot said. "We made a big deal of it, since I spell my name with one T. She said that would make me another grandmother."

"He was a precious child and she was so proud of him. She was a good mother."

Before Elliot arrived, Thomas worked as office coordinator for her husband, who shares a Matthews clinic, Carolina Nephrology Associates, with a partner, Dr. Kenneth Dunbar. The clinic specializes in kidney disorders.

Dunbar said the two had been partners about 18 months. He declined to be further interviewed.

Friedland graduated from the University of Rochester's medical school in 1981. Dr. Jared Schwartz, chief of pathology at Presbyterian Hospital, described him as "intense, really enthusiastic, young and a pretty nice guy."

Thomas met Friedland while living in Manhattan, where she managed a recording studio.

The couple moved to Miami, where Friedland completed his training at the University of Miami.

They married in Miami and moved to Charlotte in 1986. Thomas lost no time getting involved in Charlotte's NOW chapter. She had been a member of the organization since she was a student at the University of Rochester, where she earned a psychology degree.

"I was much more of an out-here kind of feminist than I am today," she recalled during an interview with The Charlotte Observer last year.

Thomas summed up today's women's movement this way: "It's become much more mainstream. We're not the radical, bra-burning, crazed feminists who want men to share 50-50 in their household work and cook three times a week.

"We're for basic rights and family and women to be able to make private decisions about how many children they want to have in their families. And that's apple pie. That's not something anyone's afraid of."

She had high hopes for her son.

"I think he's really going to be a great feminist, and he's hopefully going to be able to live a lot of things I believe and am not able to put into action because of society. I hope he feels freer."

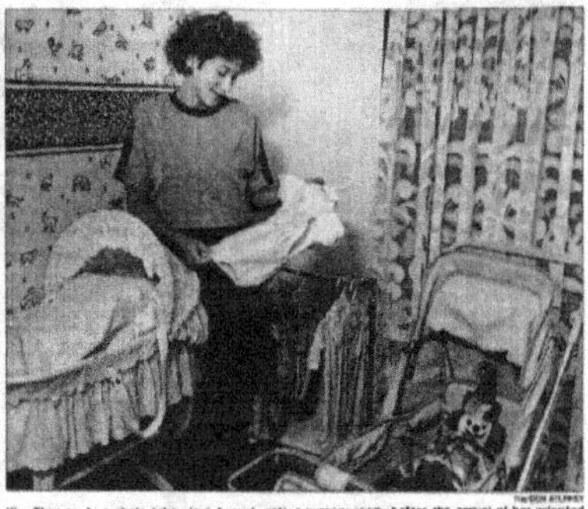

Kim Thomas, in a photo taken last August, gets a nursery ready before the arrival of her adopted child, Elliot.

Memorial Service Today

A memorial service will be at 4 p.m. today at Harry & Bryant Funeral Home. Visitation will follow.

Survivors, in addition to her husband and son, are her parents, Lewis and Helen Thomas of Westfield, N.J.; sisters, Ms. Joyce Thomas of Seattle, Ms. Lynn Thomas of Boston.

In lieu of flowers, memorials may be made to the Charlotte chapter of National Organization for Women, P.O. Box 37204, Charlotte, N.C. 28237; or to the Shelter For Battered Women, P.O. Box 220312, Charlotte, N.C. 28222.

•

Staff writer Karen Garloch contributed to this article.

Mourners Recall Woman's Warmth

Slain Activist's Family, Friends Reel From 'Great Loss'

By JOHN WILDMAN
Staff Writer

In a flower-filled chapel, 250 friends and relatives silently paid tribute Sunday to women's rights activist Kim Thomas.

About 2 miles away, police quietly spent their third day searching for clues at Thomas' home, where she was beaten to death Friday.

The Rev. Frank O'Rourke's words, at Sunday's memorial service, captured the shock of Thomas' death.

"We come together in a time of bewilderment, confusion and pain," said O'Rourke, rector of St. Patrick's Catholic Church.

"This is a great loss," he said, praising Thomas for her "warmth, her clarity of vision and her longing for dignity for all people."

After the service at Harry & Bryant Funeral Home, Dr. Edward Friedland — Thomas' husband — exchanged handshakes and hugs with the guests.

Nearby, someone else held 13-month-old Elliot, the son he and Thomas adopted about a year ago.

Friedland, a thin, dark-haired man, looked tired as friends consoled him.

A partner at a clinic for kidney patients, Friedland told police he arrived at his Churchill Road home Friday about 10 p.m. and heard Elliot crying in his crib. He found Thomas, 32, dead on the dining room floor.

Homicide investigator Jim Hollingsworth said Sunday that police "are very actively investigating the case. We are continuing to process the scene today and tonight."

Police have said Thomas apparently struggled with her attacker. Autopsy results haven't been released.

Police are asking that anyone with information about Thomas' activities Friday call Crime Stoppers at 334-1600, anytime.

Thomas and Friedland moved to Charlotte in 1986 from Miami, where she was a stockbroker and appeared as an analyst on cable television's Financial News Network.

She became a leader of the Charlotte chapter of the National Organization for Women and she co-authored a guide book for pregnant women.

Craig Madans was among the 250 people who paid tribute to Thomas Sunday. He had met her last year during his losing Charlotte mayoral campaign.

"Charlotte has lost a very strong, caring woman who fought for other people," said Madans. "It's such an absolute waste."

Victim Was Found Slashed, Bound

Police Withhold Details To Protect Case

By NANCY WEBB
Staff Writer

As details of Kim Thomas' murder emerge, the killing grows more gruesome.

Several sources revealed Monday that Thomas was found facedown on the dining room floor of her southeast Charlotte home, her throat slashed and hands bound behind her back.

Secrecy has surrounded the case from the moment investigators arrived Friday night at Thomas' home in a secluded area off Churchill Road. Police have clamped down on information in the case, saying they want to safeguard details that could make or break the case later.

Although the autopsy is complete, police officials have asked Mecklenburg medical examiner Dr. Mike Sullivan not to reveal the results.

"We don't have a prime suspect, so to speak, right now," Cmdr. Bruce Treadaway said. "We don't want to jeopardize the case."

A police report says that Thomas — a 32-year-old women's rights activist and former stockbroker — was killed with a "knife/cutting instrument." Police say they have not found the weapon.

Treadaway did reveal that police are investigating two break-ins Monday in the area near Thomas' home off Wendover Road. A nearby house on Wendwood Lane was broken into about 3:30 a.m. while the owner and his family slept inside. The intruders fled when the burglar alarm sounded.

The other break-in occurred next door to Thomas' house. A neighbor told police that someone went through her glove compartment, leaving papers lying all over the front seat of her car.

Police are investigating both incidents.

"It might be connected, it might not," Treadaway said.

Police believe Thomas likely died sometime Friday morning. Her husband, Dr. Edward Friedland, found her body.

Friedland came home from work about 10 p.m. and heard the couple's 13-month-old son, Elliot, crying. Friedland went to the child's room and took the baby from the crib, spotting his wife's body on the dining room floor as he left the child's room.

Police asked that anyone who spoke with Thomas or tried to call her Friday morning and got no answer telephone the felony investigations bureau at 336-2311 between 8 a.m. and 11 p.m. or Crime Stoppers at 334-1400 anytime.

Kim Thomas

MS. KIM THOMAS

Ms. Kim Thomas, 32, of 3853 Churchill Road, died Friday, July 27, 1990 at her residence. A native of Westfield, NJ, Ms. Thomas was born June 8, 1958. She was former Office Manager of Carolina Nephrology Associates, P.A. She was a graduate of the University of Rochester and had worked in broadcasting in Miami, FL prior to coming to Charlotte. Ms. Thomas was an active member of the National Organization of Women. She was co-author of the book "A Charlotte Child". A Memorial service was held at 4:00 P.M Sunday at Harry and Bryant Chapel in the Oaks. Reverend Francis O'Rourke of St. Patrick's Cathedral officiated. She was the beloved wife of Edward L. Friedland, beloved mother of Elliot Friedland, of the home; beloved daughter of Louis and Helen Thomas of Westfield, NJ; and beloved sister of Ms. Joyce Thomas of Seattle, WA and Ms. Lynn Thomas of Boston, MA. In lieu of flowers, Memorials may be made to the Charlotte chapter of National Organization of Women, P.O. Box 37204, Charlotte, NC 28237 or to the Shelter For Battered Women, P.O. Box 220312, Charlotte, NC 28222. Harry and Bryant Co. is serving the family of Ms. Thomas.

REWARD

Up To

$25,000^00

For information leading to the Arrest and Conviction of the killer(s) of KIM THOMAS, slain in her home, Friday, July 27, 1990, on Churchill Road, Charlotte, N.C.

Rewarded Anonymously

Offer good for information provided up to one year from Oct. 11, 1990

CALL: CRIME STOPPERS

704-334-1600

Reward Provided By Kim Thomas Reward Fund

10 years after Charlotte activist Kim Thomas was slashed to death in her home, the murder case is open – and unsolved

FRANCISCO KJOLSETH/Staff

Marjorie Storch, a friend of murder victim Kim Thomas, sits beside the memorial to Thomas in Freedom Park. The local chapter of the National Organization for Women and some Thomas family members will dedicate the plaque Nov. 4.

Park area honors Thomas

By TONY MECIA
Staff Writer

Kim Thomas, the victim in one of Charlotte's best-known and unsolved murder cases, will be remembered next week with a memorial in Freedom Park.

The local chapter of the National Organization for Women and some members of the Thomas family will dedicate the bronze plaque Nov. 4. At the time of her death in 1990, Thomas, 32, was a leader with NOW and a women's rights activist.

"We just thought this would be a nice way to remember her and do something nice for the community," said Marjorie Storch, past president of Charlotte's NOW chapter. "And it's a reminder that this is an unsolved case."

The Thomas murder case has been a source of intrigue almost since her body was found, throat slashed and hands bound behind her back, in the southeast Charlotte home she shared with her husband and 1-year-old son.

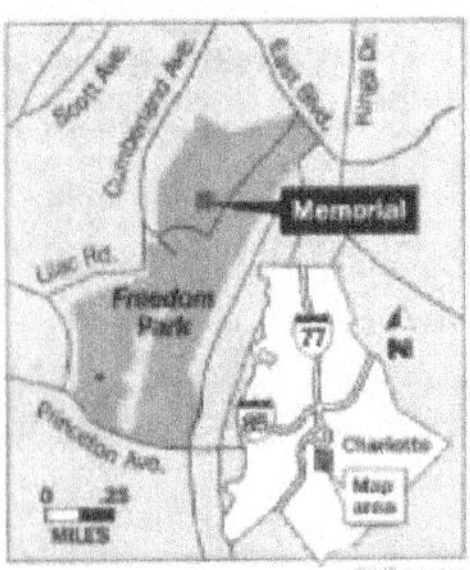

Staff graphic

Four years later, police and prosecutors charged Thomas' husband, Dr. Ed Friedland, with murder. But prosecutors dropped the charge in 1995, citing a lack of evidence.

Friedland then sued the city and four police investigators, claiming they botched the investigation, maligned him and ignored another suspect, Marion Anthony Gales, who had a history of break-ins in the area. The case against the city is expected to go to trial next year.

Friedland also sued Gales in civil court for wrongful death and won an $8.6 million judgment. Friedland has said he doesn't expect to collect the award from Gales.

Gales, 38, is serving time at the Albemarle Correctional Institution in Stanly County for an unrelated crime. Gales, who proclaims his innocence, has not been charged in Thomas' death.

In the past decade, the case has attracted the attention of national media, including NBC's "Dateline" and the syndicated tabloid show "Hard Copy."

Thomas' family members say they hope the memorial will focus attention not on the mystery surrounding her death, but on her active life.

Please see **THOMAS** / page **48**

Sister and police mark 25th year since killing

Kim Thomas was stabbed to death on July 27, 1990

She was killed in her Cotswold home

BY JOE MARUSAK
jmarusak@charlotteobserver.com

It's been 25 years since her sister, Kim Thomas, was killed in her Cotswold home, but Lynn Thomas said she's never given up hope the killer will be arrested.

"It's part of being a Thomas," Lynn Thomas told the Observer at Freedom Park on Saturday, where she marked the anniversary with friends of her sister, and police investigating the death. "You don't give up. It's just not an option. Somebody said to me, 'Is this going to put you in any kind of danger?' If it did, so what? I'll handle it. I'm not going to shrink away."

Kim Thomas died on July 27, 1990, stabbed more than 20 times. She was 32. Her son, Elliot, was 10 months old and in his crib. He was unharmed. It's one of Charlotte's most high-profile unsolved murders.

Thomas' husband, kidney surgeon Dr. Ed Friedland, who now lives in Florida, was charged in 1994 with the killing. Police contended Friedland killed Thomas as a way out of their marriage, but the charge was later dismissed because of insufficient evidence.

Marion Anthony Gales, who did yard work for Thomas, was another suspect. He denied that he committed the crime. Police never charged him.

But Friedland filed a wrongful death lawsuit in civil court against Gales, alleging that Gales had killed his wife. A jury in 1997 agreed and ordered Gales to pay Friedland $8.6 million.

Gales is in prison for voluntary manslaughter in the death of LaCoya Monique Martin, whose shirtless body was found face down beside a house on Oaklawn Avenue in Charlotte on April 6, 2008. He will remain behind bars until 2025.

The Charlotte-Mecklenburg Police Department's Cold Case Unit is investigating Thomas' death.

K. Thomas

Lynn Thomas said she was glad police were at the park Saturday to help mark the anniversary.

"We're following up on many different leads," Sgt. Darrell Price of the Cold Case Unit said at a news conference where Lynn Thomas displayed poster boards full of photos of her sister. Price said he couldn't go into details about any suspects, "but what I can tell you is that we are moving forward with the investigation."

Having different detectives in the cold case unit from a decade ago means having "a brand new set of eyes looking at everything," Price said.Lynn Thomas said she's more optimistic than ever the case will be resolved. She spoke to the media near a bronze plaque that honors her sister as "an activist for good causes."

"My family and friends have persistently been working with the police to resolve this," said Lynn Thomas, who was 34 when her sister died. "I'm the most optimistic I've felt in years. No new information per se, but they're looking at it from a different perspective, and I hope it will come to a resolution very soon."

She will never give up, she said, for the sister she loved "more than anybody else on the planet."

Joe Marusak:
704-358-5067, @jmarusak

Friedland murder charge dropped

Doctor declares his innocence

By MARY ELIZABETH DeANGELIS
Staff Writer

Dr. Edward Friedland ended four years of silence Tuesday, insisting he did not kill Kim Thomas.

"I am innocent," he said. "I had nothing to do with Kim's death. There is nothing that would benefit me more than having whoever killed Kim brought to justice."

Friedland has spent the years since his first wife's death as one of Charlotte's most well-known murder suspects. His face and name and details of the case appeared frequently in the newspaper and on television.

When he'd go to a store or to pick up his child at school, strangers stared. People he didn't know speculated, "Do you think he did it?"

"I can't imagine anybody in Charlotte has ever been investigated more than I have," he said in an interview Tuesday night, hours after prosecutors dropped the murder charge against him.

Please see Friedland/page 10A

Dr. Edward Friedland

Prosecutor: Too little evidence

By KATHLEEN McCLAIN
Staff Writer

In a startling move Tuesday, prosecutors dropped a first-degree murder charge against Dr. Edward Friedland, leaving unsolved the 1990 slashing death of his first wife, Kim Thomas.

Prosecutor Richard Gordon told a judge in a pretrial hearing that the district attorney's office had re-evaluated the case and decided there wasn't enough evidence to try the Charlotte kidney specialist.

Gordon said the decision was based on a crucial ruling last week that would have kept a New York forensic pathologist from telling jurors that Thomas "most likely" was killed before 7:30 a.m., the time her husband told police he left for work.

The testimony of Dr. Michael Baden, medical examiner for the New York State Police, was vital to prosecutors seeking the death penalty in a case with no murder weapon, no eyewitnesses and no matches for hair, fingerprints and shoe prints found at the blood-drenched scene.

Still, Gordon's brief announcement shocked on-lookers prepared to hear final arguments from defense lawyers who said police waited too long — four

Please see Thomas/page 10A

10A THE CHARLOTTE OBSERVER Wednesday, March 29, 1995

BOB LEVERONE/Staff

Attorney David Rudolf explains what he thinks went wrong in investigating Dr. Edward Friedland in the murder of his wife Kim Thomas. "You didn't hear the district attorney talking about technicalities. What the district attorney talked about was lack of evidence . . . ," Rudolf said. Sitting next to Rudolf is investigator Ron Guerette of Guerette Investigations of Charlotte.

Doctor relied on support of friends

Friedland

Continued from page 1A

"It was a relief, after 4½ years, of what I've had to go through, and my family had to go through that once it got out on the table it had to be dismissed."

Thomas' death brought many changes for Friedland. He sold the home he and Thomas shared, then bought another. He remarried, and he and his wife Lisa have since had two children together. Friedland already had a son from his marriage to Thomas; Lisa Friedland had a son from a previous relationship.

After his arrest last July, Friedland gave up his medical practice. He says he doesn't know what he's going to do from here but will talk things over with his family and make a decision.

So how has he gotten through the past four years?

"When you're standing up for something that's right, it gives you a lot of strength," he said.

"The people who we see regularly have been supportive," he said. As for as strangers' speculation, "I'm innocent, therefore, I'm not ashamed to be seen, and won't be in the future."

Still, he knows that some, including Thomas' family, won't accept his innocence.

"It hurts, it always hurt, and it still hurts," he said.

"As sure as the sun rises in the east and sets in the west, I had absolutely nothing to do with Kim's death," Friedland said. "Today was a day of justice for Kim, it was a good day for Kim.

"It just hurts me that some people out there don't believe that."

He said that for the first time since Thomas death, he feels like he's gotten a chance to defend himself.

"I've been in a position where I've had to put up with the innuendo, and the half-truths," he said.

"It's my hope that as people come to understand why this case was dropped, they'll understand the answer to the tragedy does not lie with me."

Details about the Kim Thomas murder case

- **July 27, 1990:** Kim Thomas is found handcuffed and slashed to death in the dining room of the Churchill Road home she shared with her husband, Dr. Edward Friedland.
- **Aug. 10, 1990:** Police say they don't think Thomas' killer will kill again.
- **Aug. 22, 1990:** Speaking to reporters for the first time, Friedland asks the public to come forward with information about the case.
- **Oct. 9, 1990:** Friedland announces a private $25,000 reward fund started by Thomas' family and friends.
- **Oct. 19, 1990:** Friedland says police have told him he is a suspect.
- **June 25, 1991:** Thomas' parents, Lou and Helen Thomas, and her sisters, Joyce and Lynn Thomas, meet with Charlotte police and issue a public plea for more information.
- **July 27, 1991:** Thomas is honored at a community memorial service sponsored by the Charlotte chapter of the National Organization for Women. Friedland attends.
- **Sept. 27, 1993:** Prosecutors file for a court order to review N.C. tax records for Thomas, Friedland and his medical practice, saying the information "may provide evidence to prove motive" in the murder case.
- **July 12, 1994:** Friedland arrested, charged with murder, then freed on $300,000 bond.
- **Sept. 8, 1994:** Friedland resigns from his medical practice, Carolina Nephrology Associates, saying he wants to "devote his time to personal needs and his family."
- **Oct. 12, 1994:** Friedland pleads not guilty.
- **March 20, 1995:** At a pretrial hearing, forensic pathologist Dr. Michael Baden says he believes it's "more likely" Thomas died before 7:30 a.m., the time Friedland says he last saw her alive.
- **March 22, 1995:** A judge rules Baden can only testify about scientific data: he may not say one time is more likely than another.
- **March 28, 1995:** Prosecution drops charge against Friedland.

Prosecution drops murder charge

Thomas

Continued from page 1A

years — to charge Friedland in the July 27, 1990, killing.

Friedland, clearly caught off guard, cast a puzzled look at his wife, Lisa. She smiled slowly as Gordon said: "That will conclude the business before the court in this case."

Moments later, Friedland embraced his mother, his wife, his sister-in-law and other friends who had gathered in court Tuesday and during last week's preliminary hearing.

"There was justice done today," he said.

In an interview from his home Tuesday evening Friedland, 38, denied being involved with Thomas' death. "The evidence has never been there, and it never will be there because I had nothing to do with Kim's death. I am innocent."

After the hearing, Lisa Friedland was literally shaking with relief.

"I don't even know what to say," she said, dabbing tears from her eyes. "I can't believe it happened so fast. What they just said — it still hasn't really dawned on me."

The murder victim's father, reached at his home in New Jersey, said Friedland is "lucky to live in a country where the legal system has such a high standard for proof beyond a reasonable doubt."

Lou Thomas said he had no complaints with either prosecutors or police officers assigned to investigate his daughter's death.

"What happened today means Dr. Friedland is relieved of all charges right now, but that still leaves things open," he said. "I'll quote Yogi Berra: 'It's not over 'til it's over.'"

There is no statute of limitations on murder in North Carolina. Because the prosecution's case against Friedland was dropped at this stage, he could be charged again if enough admissible evidence surfaces.

Kim Thomas: The brutality of her murder shocked Charlotte.

Kim Thomas, a 32-year-old writer and former stockbroker, was found handcuffed and slashed to death on the dining room floor in the couple's home off Wendover Road. Their 10-month-old son was crying in his crib down the hall.

Friedland told police Thomas was alive when he left for work shortly after 7:30 a.m. the day of the murder. He said he found her body when he returned from work at 10 p.m.

The brutality of the killing shocked Charlotte. Police told reporters the crime apparently was not committed by someone who would strike again and called a meeting to calm worried neighbors in the Wendover Hills area.

Within a few days, Friedland hired Charlotte attorney Mike Scofield and private investigator Ron Guerette. Within three months, he said police had told him he was a suspect.

No charges were filed until last July, when Friedland was indicted, arrested and charged with murder. He was freed on $300,000 and pleaded not guilty in October.

Friedland's new attorney David Rudolf of Chapel Hill came to court this month with motions asking Superior Court Judge Marvin Gray to dismiss the case and to suppress Baden's expert testimony about the time Thomas died.

Baden was hired by Charlotte-Mecklenburg police in July 1993 to review autopsy findings and details of the police investigation.

Last week, Baden told the judge it was "more likely (Thomas) died before 7:30 a.m. rather than after." But he said he arrived at that opinion by studying anecdotal, as well as scientific, evidence.

He testified that Thomas hadn't changed out of her night clothes and hadn't drunk coffee or eaten breakfast within a couple of hours of her death. He said she was still wearing one of the earrings she normally wore to sleep; her baby hadn't been tended to and the family dog apparently had been kept in the baby's room all day.

Rudolf said police brought the New Yorker in because neither Mecklenburg Medical Examiner Michael Sullivan nor N.C. Medical Examiner John Butts would narrow the probable time of death precisely enough to support their theory that Friedland killed his wife.

The defense lawyer argued — successfully — that factors not related specifically to scientific indicators of when Thomas died should not be allowed at trial. Gray ruled in Friedland's favor, shooting down the prosecution's best available evidence.

Tuesday, Rudolf renewed his argument that police had ignored a more likely suspect, a handyman from nearby Cotter Heights, while pursuing evidence about Friedland.

"What happened in court today is justice being served," Rudolf said on the courthouse steps. "You didn't hear the district attorney talking about technicalities. What the district attorney talked about was lack of evidence . . .

"It's amazing that the authorities could go so far with a capital case against a person who has never done anything wrong."

At a news conference, Rudolf handed over stacks of police records that he said documented evidence against the second suspect — a man with a criminal record who had done odd jobs at the Friedland home. He said the man owned a pair of handcuffs virtually identical to those found on Thomas' wrists.

The lawyer said he didn't think police had a vendetta against Friedland, but said investigators failed to share information and follow important leads.

"The fact that there's no evidence (to try Friedland) after 4½ or five years ought to say something . . . ," Rudolf said. "I would submit to you that's exoneration. The fact that there's no evidence indicates he's innocent."

Charlotte-Mecklenburg Police Deputy Chief Larry Snider said the department still considers the Thomas murder an open investigation.

"There could be prosecution at some point," Snider said. "We could not comment on any of the investigation or any of the suspects we've investigated."

Mecklenburg District Attorney Peter Gilchrist said police had worked diligently to track down Thomas' killer. He urged anyone who has information about the case to call CrimeStoppers at (704) 334-1600.

Staff writer Mary Elizabeth DeAngelis contributed to this article.

The Garden of Peace, Boston, MA

Freedom Park, Charlotte, NC

Made in the USA
Coppell, TX
01 June 2022

78373588R00155